Y0-EKS-677

ADVENTURING WITH GOD

ADVENTURING WITH GOD

by

Elbert A. Dempsey, Jr.

An Adult Study Course

Christian Education Commission
Reorganized Church of Jesus Christ of Latter Day Saints

Copyright © 1985
Herald House
Independence, Missouri
Printed in the United States of America

All rights in this book are reserved. No part of the text may be reproduced in any form without written permission of the publishers, except brief quotations used in connection with reviews in magazines or newspapers.

95 94 93   5 6 7

CONTENTS

PREFACE

Adventuring with God **has two purposes:**
First Purpose: to help people maintain a dynamic faith in a time of confusion

A crisis of faith challenges religions centered on a personal God. These factors contribute to this crisis:
1. Scripture is seemingly discredited.

A convincing body of evidence suggests that
- creation occurred very differently from the interpretation of the Bible authors;
- the return of Israel to Jerusalem after the Babylonian captivity was not as glorious as scripture predicted;
- the gospel stories are not eyewitness accounts.

Numerous such examples disturb many people who base their faith on a literal view of scripture.

2. God is doubted by many.

Dazzling victories of human knowledge make God seem irrelevant to many. For example, human effort eliminated the scourge of smallpox. This vaccine created through scientific efforts saves more lives each year than are claimed by all known faith healers.

3. People seek and find nothing.

Most damaging of all to one's faith may be unrewarding personal experience. A person prays earnestly and feels that nothing happens. A parent watches a child suffer innocently, painfully, futilely. Another person senses loneliness in the struggle against remorseless fate. Each wonders how a loving God can ignore such personal devastation.

Some persons respond to these threats to their faith by clinging tenaciously to tradition. They are certain God is creator and ruler of the universe. They are certain the Bible is God's true word. Any evidence to the contrary is assumed to be false. This closed-minded and uncompromising stance works only if the individuals reject all conflicting evidence, whether it appears false or true. This rigidity eliminates growth as well as wavering. It frequently leads to unrealistic positions and hastens the exodus of other people who find no appeal in such unrealistic views.

Experience indicates that a more effective approach to these threats is to focus on the third threat and equip people for a rewarding personal experience with God. This is the thrust of this book.

When we develop a satisfactory working relationship with God, the big faith issues can be dealt with effectively. For example, we will be confident that however creation occurred, God was at the center. We will then be secure enough to confront conflicting evidence on its merits. If we find truth, we can welcome it as clarifying our faith, not threatening our faith. Then, and only then, faith becomes simultaneously dynamic, realistic, productive, and strong.

Second Purpose: to encourage people toward mission as God's partners

The Restoration church is commissioned to build Zion. As members we are to be instruments in fulfilling part of the Lord's Prayer, "Thy kingdom come. Thy will be done as in heaven, so in earth" (Luke 11:2 IV). The following factors interfere with this crucial mission:

1. Some members have become a waiting people in a waiting church.

   Many wait for the glorious day when the spiritual endowment comes or when the Lord will redeem Zion. Many have become too comfortable with remote, deferred dreams.

2. Some members have unrealistic spiritual expectations.

   They assume that when church members become pure enough, God will pour ideas into their heads and use them in remarkable ways. They are overly dependent on God to provide the initiative and results.

3. Some members are prisoners of past interpretations.

   Their rigid dependence on tradition prevents them from being a prophetic people who can grow to be God's effective agents in their time and place.

4. Some members do not try because it looks hopeless.

   They may lack faith in God. They may lack faith in the church. They may lack faith in themselves. Whatever the reason, they do not try because they are discouraged.

This book counters these four problems. It presents a call for us to be active partners with God. Here is guidance on how to achieve a fruitful partnership. These insights are crucial to prepare us for effective mission.

*   *   *   *   *

This book contains heavy use of the first person plural: we, us, our. This is important. The wonderful promises (and warnings) of God apply to us all. God seeks to work personally with you. . . and me. . . and our friends. . . and our enemies.

Elbert A. Dempsey, Jr.

HOW TO USE THIS COURSE

Ideas for the Teacher

1. One major problem in church school is that many students do not study. Incentives have been tried with modest results. This course has been designed to be effective with or without outside study. The author makes heavy use of the students' experiences. Other necessary background material is to be presented during class. Books may even be kept in the classroom.

2. The course contains three categories of material:
   a. Material for class reading. Assign students who are comfortable with public reading to read it. When this sign (#) appears, a different student may be assigned to read what follows. This sign emphasizes different points. Assign all parts in a series before the reading starts.
   b. Points for class discussion. The teacher may read these. They may be either questions or statements. They look like this:
   Q 1. These may also call for written responses by students. Some teachers may like to use this text like an activity book with students writing responses and then sharing with the class or in discussion groups.
   c. Discussion comments. These are found at the end of each session. Urge the students to wrestle with the question before looking at the author's response.

11

3. Help students keep an open mind as they move toward mature perceptions. As teacher, you may provide probing questions or evidence to focus the discussion. Avoid saying, "Here is the right answer." The comments suggested at the end cover only some of the author's ideas. Encourage exploration of other possibilities.
4. Cover the material in sequence. The material for class reading is intended to lead into the question that follows. Unlike most books, the text often does not include the most important insights because the students should develop these themselves. Students' comments will help you lead the discussion in a certain direction. This makes it very important to explore what is said about each question before moving on in the text.
5. The session is its own lesson plan. You may add illustrations or questions that will help your particular class. However, you may find it easy to go through the material in the order it is presented.
6. Prepare in advance.
   This is unusually easy because the basic lesson planning and outside research have been done for you. Still, preparation is important.
   a. Read the session to feel the flow and be sure you understand the concepts well.
   b. Note special stories or quotes you may want to add.
   c. Invite any resource persons you may need to enrich the experience.
   d. After working each discussion question on your own, study the comments at the end of the session. Plan how you can help the students develop those insights without reading the "answer."

Ideas for the Individual Student

Feel free to read this text as you would any other book with these important differences:

1. Stop when you come to each discussion question. Consider it from two or three different vantage points. Develop your own response.
2. Next, look at the comments for that question at the end of the session. Avoid looking at them before you have had a chance to develop your own ideas.
3. After you read the author's comments, explore how you agree or disagree and why. Then go on with the next question or text.

THE HOLY STRENGTHENER

KEY CONCEPT: A Personal God

KEY STATEMENT: The most meaningful adventure this life offers is the discovery that we are in partnership with God.

OBJECTIVES

At the end of the session you should be able to
1. explain circumstances in which God can bless us personally;
2. identify an incident when God moved in each of our personal lives;
3. explain the role of spiritual gifts.

Hazel Withee, one of the church's fine organists, now deceased, told an instructive story of her family's conversion. Her grandmother, Cornelia, was Dutch. She was full of questions about the meaning of life, God's purpose in her, and many things that seemed significant. When Cornelia would go to her minister for answers his reply would be, "That is not given you to know, my child."

Eventually Cornelia married Lambertus Niedorp, a young man of like mind. Shortly after their marriage they decided to go to the United States to find a more meaningful life.

They crossed the Atlantic in the same ship on which Apostle James Caffall was returning from one of his missions to England. During the voyage, he conducted

Apostle
James
Caffall

services on the ship. As he preached in English, this young Dutch couple, who spoke no English, discovered to their amazement that they understood. He raised and answered some of the questions to which they had been denied answers. Cornelia and Lambertus discovered to their great joy, "It *is* given you to know, my child." The results are meaningful. A century later, their grandchildren and great-grandchildren lead productive lives directed toward strengthening Zion. Their great-great-grandchildren are being reared in the life the Niedorps left Holland to find.

But we should not be too surprised. God worked like that in those days.

\# Much more recently, the United States Army stationed Caffall's great-grandson, Jerry Dempsey, in Korea. Some young RLDS men had just organized a group of converts among the Koreans. After Jerry arrived, the other Americans were transferred away. Jerry was the only priesthood member to minister to this group of converts. He could speak no Korean. They could speak little English. They organized a class to study conversational English but it did not go well. Jerry feared the work would fall apart because of his inadequacy.

It well could have. However, to their amazement, the Koreans discovered that in Sunday services when Jerry spoke in English they often understood. When they spoke in Korean, Jerry often understood. In his soft-spoken way, Jerry said, "We often felt the Holy Spirit was a bridge to understanding. It happened so consistently we came to expect it. For over a year whenever we had important business to transact, or important truths to explore, we understood each other beyond our vocabularies." It's the same experience his great-grandfather had, except it happened not once on a ship, but repeatedly for fourteen months.

But we should not be too surprised. God works like that today.

\# Ancient Judah celebrated the revelation of the Ten Commandments on the day of Pentecost. It was so important that devout Jews from many lands made the pilgrimage to Jerusalem every year. The first day of Pentecost after the resurrection of Christ is often called the birthday of the Christian church. A small band of followers of Jesus were gathered in Jerusalem. Then a remarkable experience transformed this bewildered little group into a dynamic force that resulted in the baptism of three thousand converts the first day and eventually transformed the world.

And when the day of Pentecost was fully come, they were all with one accord in one place.... And they were all filled with the Holy Ghost, and began to speak with other tongues, as the Spirit gave them utterance. And there were dwelling at Jerusalem Jews, devout men, out of every nation under heaven. Now when this was noised abroad, the multitude came together, and were confounded, because that every man heard them speak in his own language. And they were all amazed and marveled, saying one to another, Behold, are not all these which speak Galileans? And how hear we every man in our own tongue, wherein we were born? Parthians, and Medes, and Elamites, and the dwellers in Mesopotamia, and in Judea, and Cappadocia, in Pontus, and Asia,...Cretes and Arabians, we do hear them speak in our tongues the wonderful works of God. And they were all amazed, and were in doubt, saying one to another, What meaneth this?—Acts 2:1, 4-9, 11, 12 IV

Q 1 What gift is demonstrated in all three stories?

Q 2 When we realize God moves among us today just as in Bible times, how does this knowledge

a. *make us feel closer to the religious leaders of the Bible?*
   b. *give us hope in meeting the problems of life?*

Q 3 Why did the blessings occur?

Q 4 How are the experiences applicable to our lives?

\#   God's Many Blessings

Shirley Smith of Odessa, Missouri, wrote about the most devastating year of her life. Just as she recovered from surgery her parents and her husband's parents became gravely ill. There was the strain of dragging three small children to three widely separated hospitals almost every day for months. There were months of caring for bedfast parents in her home and theirs at the same time. There was the anguish of watching her mother slowly die.

When it was over, Shirley was totally spent. She recoiled from the thought of any responsibility outside her home.

At Communion service the pastor announced, "People, I can't find anyone who will take the Skylark girls' group."

Shirley reports,

When he said these words, the good Spirit made it known to me that this was where I was to work. There was no time for me to *rest* in the Lord's work. I was also assured that God would strengthen me for this task just as I had been sustained during the recent trials.

I took the job, and experienced marvelous ministry from the Skylark girls. . . . At our Thanksgiving meeting as we ended with our circle prayer, every girl prayed in her own way. Many of them said, "Thank you, Lord, for Shirley. We're so glad she comes and shares her love with us." I was also grateful to tell them through my prayer: "Thank you, Lord, for each one of these beautiful girls. Only you could have known how much I needed their pure, sincere love and joy."—*Restoration Witness*, September 1982.

Q 3 Why did the blessings occur?

Q 4 How can the experiences be applicable to our lives?

\# The most meaningful, and one of the most exciting, adventures of this life is to discover we are in partnership with the divine.

In the drama-packed scene as Jesus ate with the twelve for the last time before his crucifixion, he promised:

> And I will pray to the Father, and he shall give you another Comforter, that he may abide with you forever; Even the Spirit of truth; whom the world cannot receive, because it seeth him not, neither knoweth him; but ye know him; for he dwelleth with you, and shall be in you.—John 14:16-17 IV

Comforter is translated from the Latin *con fortare.* This is from the same root as fortissimo or fortify. It meant "with strength." What Jesus said was he would send a holy strengthener.

In English the word has more recently come to mean a solace in time of grief. Jesus certainly meant that, but early Christian authors suggest that he meant a great deal more. He offered divine strength of *any* needed variety in developing a godly life or in achieving God's purposes.

Before class the teacher has invited two people (not necessarily members of the class) to tell about one meaningful spiritual experience in their lives. Each will illustrate one of the following:

Ways God Blesses Us

When I am troubled—peace of mind
When I am fearful—courage
When I am confused—understanding
When I am petty—bigness
When I am injured—healing

When I am discouraged—hope
When I am blocked—a way to progress
When I am rejected—love

They are to explain these four elements in their experience:
a. The need which the blessing met
b. How the story developed
c. How God was involved
d. The results of the incident

Be sure the guests understand that they are not to philosophize. Instead, they need to tell a true story about which the class may philosophize. If the guests want to share their concept of spirituality, they may do so after class members discuss their experiences.

After each story discuss these questions:

Q 3 Why did the blessings occur?

Q 4 How can the experiences be applicable to our lives?

If there is time, invite class members to share experiences where blessings were received which were different from those reported previously.

After each story, repeat questions 3 and 4.

KEY INSIGHTS

Write below your personal beliefs on these subjects. Discuss these in class to stimulate ideas before writing personal comments. However, do not try to arrive at a consensus. Write what you personally feel. These beliefs will be reviewed in session 7.

1. How ready is God to provide blessings?

2. In what circumstances does God provide blessings?

3. How can we tell if it is really God acting?

DISCUSSION COMMENTS

1. **What gift is demonstrated in all three stories?**
These stories involve the gift of interpretation of tongues.

2. **When we realize that God moves among us today just as in Bible times, how does this knowledge**
   a. **make us feel closer to the religious leaders of the Bible?**
   There is no one right answer to the two parts of this question. The important thing is to help each other think through how the knowledge that God is involved with us in remarkable ways affects our personal outlooks in each of these areas. We might feel closer to biblical religious leaders when we
   - realize that God really can work as some of their stories tell us. With this realization they and their stories become more meaningful to us.
   - see parallels to what happens today in their trials and triumphs.
   - recognize that they were ordinary people like ourselves who worked with God the same as we do.

   b. **give us hope in meeting the problems of life?**
   While this can properly mean different things to each of us, there is comfort in knowing that we are not alone in confronting life. Whatever our need, God is available to help as remarkably as at any time in the past.

3. **Why did the blessings occur?**
We explore this further in following sessions. Expert answers are not needed at this time.

However, we may observe in each story that there was a real need. Each blessing served an important purpose. Each time there was a person who could respond to the spiritual guidance and was edified because of the event. Discuss evidence of these in each story.

4. **How are the experiences applicable to our lives?**
   We can explore several directions on this. Perhaps we can see a different direction with each experience on which this question is repeated. Here are some possible directions:
   • Does it indicate a virtue we need to develop?
   • Does it demonstrate the importance of faith?
   • Does it show God's love for us?
   • Does it show the need to love others?
   • Does it give us hope or joy?

THE MANY WAYS OF GOD

SESSION 2

KEY CONCEPT: Spiritual Gifts

KEY STATEMENT: God can help us in ways as diverse as our needs.

OBJECTIVES

At the end of the session you should be able to
1. describe the diversity of spiritual gifts;
2. list nine or more types of spiritual gifts;
3. explain the nature and value of four classes of gifts;
4. explain why we should not overemphasize lists and categories of gifts;
5. discuss the tension between the belief that all things are spiritual and the claim that some experiences are not spiritual.

DIVERSITIES OF SPIRITUAL GIFTS

Now there are diversities of gifts, but the same Spirit. . . .For to one is given by the Spirit the word of wisdom; to another the word of knowledge by the same Spirit; to another faith by the same Spirit; to another the gifts of healing by the same Spirit; to another the working of miracles; to another prophecy; to another discerning of spirits; to another divers kinds of tongues; to another the interpretation of tongues.—I Corinthians 12:4, 8-10 IV

Paul, in his letters, lists over twenty gifts. God meets our needs in whatever way is most appropriate. The varieties of gifts are as diverse and numerous as our needs and personalities.

Q 1 What kinds of needs might God meet with a spiritual gift?

Q 2 What kinds of needs might God not meet with a spiritual gift?

CLASSIFICATION OF SPIRITUAL GIFTS

If we, as disciples, would deal with these gifts wisely, we must understand the different roles of different types of gifts. President John Garver in his 1946 lectures to church appointees analyzed the Apostle Paul's list in I Corinthians 12:4, 8-10 IV. President Garver suggested three classes of gift:

1. *Major Gifts:* wisdom, knowledge, faith, discernment

2. *Minor Gifts:* prophecy, tongues, interpretation of tongues

3. *Incidental Gifts:* healing, miracles

This classification has helped our understanding of how to deal more realistically with different types of gifts, especially in focusing attention on the need for the major gifts to control the expression of the others.

Interestingly President F. Henry Edwards, who helped John Garver develop the list in 1946, is foremost

among those who think that the list served its purpose and we should now take a broader look. There is a growing feeling among many members that a fresh look at spiritual gifts is needed. This is not a call for a new look because in some ways it brings us closer to what Paul was trying to accomplish almost two thousand years ago. Here are three areas where added emphasis is needed:

\# 1. The statement should make clear that spiritual gifts can be of infinite variety. F. Henry Edwards offered this thought for the development of this session:

> Down the years we have been plagued by references to the Corinthian letter, as though the nine gifts mentioned by Paul are somehow basic as a carefully complete group. This is be-

President
F. Henry
Edwards

ing continued by some who are pushing for the renewal of the gifts at the present time. As a matter of fact there is very little warrant for this. Many other gifts are mentioned elsewhere. Some are very basic.

2. Our labels should be more descriptive and less judgmental. For example, persons who have had a miraculous conversion experience do not like to think of it as an "incidental" gift. It turned their lives around and is the basis through which "major" gifts have come. Persons whose lives have been saved by a gift of healing may properly consider it the most marvelous display of God's power they ever experienced, hardly incidental. Edwards strongly questions the "minor" label for a gift of such fundamental importance as prophecy. He feels that where prophecy and tongues are both called "minor" some might assume they are of roughly equal value. The Apostle Paul in I Corinthians 14 and our own church's experience make it clear that prophecy is a more significant gift.

3. Sometimes the Spirit strengthens us in our own personal preaching or pastoring. These abilities were reported as gifts of the Spirit in Romans 12:6-8 and Ephesians 4:11. Our list should include such skills.

The following meets these three concerns. Keep in mind that more gifts could be added. There are so many ways God can bless us that no list can be complete.

I propose four classes of gifts. The Apostle Paul is our principal source for those listed under each class, although a few are added as a reminder that no list is complete.

The church is indebted to President Maurice Draper for his insightful analysis of the characteristics of the major classes of gifts. The comments in the second and third columns are adapted from Draper's *The Gifts and Fruit of the Spirit*, Herald House, 1969.

CLASSES OF GIFTS

 # Primary Gifts   Godly personal   Ends in themselves
Wisdom   qualities
Knowledge
Faith
Discernment
Love
Kindness

 # Skill Gifts   Abilities to offer   Ends in themselves
Teaching   a more effective
Pastoring   discipleship
Serving
Witnessing
Healing
Interceding
Parenting
Singing

 # Growth Gifts   Messages which con-   Means toward
Prophecy   tribute insight to   ends
Tongues and   primary or skill gifts
  their
  interpretation
Dreams
Visions

 # Enabling   Events (usually   Means toward
  Gifts   physical) to meet   ends
Healing   specific needs to
Miracles   enable us to proceed

Gifts are of God. If you have a talent for teaching, that is fortunate. If you cultivate that talent, that is laudable. However, it does not qualify as a spiritual gift unless you can see specific ways that the Holy Spirit magnified your abilities, strengthened your dedication, or in some other way enriched you for the task.

All gifts are equally of God. Any gift is as important as the situation dictates.

Q 3 What class of gift is involved in each of the three stories at the beginning of Session 1?

Q 4 List two advantages that gifts of the growth class might have over gifts of the other classes in illustrating the blessings of the Holy Spirit?

a. _____

b. _____

Q 5 Why might we say the primary and skill gifts are "ends in themselves" while the others are not?

_____

_____

Q 6 What might be the logic of listing the gift of healing as both a skill gift and an enabling gift?

_____

_____

Q 7 *Rank the four classes according to how strongly the description applies.*

Most closely reflects the nature of God	Most spectacular
a. _____	_____
b. _____	_____
c. _____	_____
d. _____	_____

Q 8 *In each of the four classes, describe one experience in which a gift was received. Evaluate each experience to determine which type of gift it was.*

Q 9 *What are some reasons for wanting gifts of each class? Share what you have listed with another class member or the total group.*

Primary Gifts

Skill Gifts

Enabling Gifts

Q 10 *What are some dangers of seeking growth or enabling gifts without having the primary gifts firmly in control of the experience?*

DO NOT TAKE THIS LESSON TOO SERIOUSLY

This emphasis on classifiying various spiritual gifts may strike some as mechanical or simplistic. If we get too involved in categories and definitions, this is a real danger. Partly because of this, it has become increasingly fashionable to avoid any discussion of categories of gifts.

However, religious leaders of the first century and the twentieth had two good reasons to mention categories of spiritual gifts:

1. To illustrate how numerous are the ways God's grace can bless us.
2. To help people distinguish the primary gifts from the more spectacular. This is important in equipping us to guard against the abuse of the spectacular gifts and in stressing cultivation of the primary gifts, such as wisdom and love.

Several times in future sessions, the distinctions made in this lesson will be helpful. However, we should not get too involved in "playing games" with categories. There is little benefit in being too concerned with precise definitions. Once you are familiar with the basic ideas, move on.

IN ALL AND THROUGH ALL

We have discussed that some experiences are spiritual, others are not. How should we balance that against this important teaching of the church?

He that ascended up on high, as also he descended below all things, in that he comprehended all things, that he might be in all and through all things, the light of truth, which truth shineth. This is the light of Christ.

As also he is in the sun. . . . As also he is in the moon. . . . As also the light of the stars. . . . And the earth also, and the power thereof, even the earth upon which you stand.

And the light which now shineth, which giveth you light, is through him who enlighteneth your eyes, which is the same light that quickeneth your understandings; which light proceedeth forth from the presence of God, to fill the immensity of space.—Doctrine and Covenants 85:2b-f, 3a

This idea that God is in all things is a cherished insight of the church. It is sometimes expressed: "All things are spiritual."

Modern understanding about the essential unity of the universe makes this passage even more compelling than it seemed when Joseph Smith presented it in 1832.

So how can we reconcile a teaching that God is in all things with a teaching that God is not in all?

When people say God is in all things they mean such things as all history is one complex series of events and God is involved; there is just one cause-and-effect series leading to each result and God is in it; there is no separated otherworldly orbit in which God functions; the physicist deals with things of God just as surely as the theologian.

While every event involves God in the above sense, only occasionally do we humans recognize a more personal or self-conscious disclosure of God's activity. This more personal evidence of God's presence is what people commonly call a *spiritual* experience. In this book, we try to be true to both of these meanings.

a. When we speak of the spiritual (or God's involvement), we speak of these special occasions when we sense a direct and personal evidence of the wisdom, love, or power of God.

b. These experiences do not imply that God was not previously involved or that there was an intervention from outside the natural order. These special occasions are when the God who was always there appears more evident, personal, and explicit.

Q 11 How would the teaching of Doctrine and Covenants 85:2 and 3 that God is involved in all things affect one's attitude toward the following situations?

a. Sue is tempted to cheat on an exam; no one would know.

b. Eric is sent into battle for the first time.

c. Gloria is urged by her friends to go on a beer party she has objections to.

d. Bill is anxiously awaiting word on whether his tumor is malignant.

e. Jenny is having a real struggle to build up the choir to enrich church services.

Q 12 How does it affect prayer to realize we are not really inviting God to come, but are trying to open our own eyes to the God who is already there?

KEY INSIGHTS

There is no limit to the types of gifts the Spirit can provide. They are as diverse as our needs.

All spiritual gifts are of God. Yet different types have different uses, and often different values. Some are dependent on others.

The least dramatic, but most vital and enduring gifts are the primary gifts of God-like qualities such as wisdom, knowledge, faith, discernment, love, and kindness.

Spectacular gifts such as prophecy, tongues, healing, and miracles can often meet great needs and be occasions of spiritual power. However, the same gifts can be dangerously abused if the primary gifts are not firmly in control of the experience.

God is involved at all times in all situations. However, the term *spiritual* in this book refers only to those special times when a person senses an explicit and personal evidence of the wisdom, love, or power of God.

DISCUSSION COMMENTS

1. What kinds of needs might God meet with a spiritual gift?

Spiritual gifts can be used to meet any kind of need that will help us become better persons, improve our health, or help us handle a worthwhile responsibility. There is no limit to the kinds of needs God will help us meet, provided they meet godly purposes.

2. **What kinds of needs might God not meet with a spiritual gift?**

   Usually, an obvious spiritual experience will not occur to meet a need which we should meet normally. Such help could make us unnecessarily dependent and prevent our growth.

   We should not expect a blessing if a desired gift would serve a short-range purpose and would not be a good thing over the long term.

   We should not expect a blessing when the desired blessing serves a selfish desire, and does not contribute to a worthy purpose in ourselves or in others.

3. **What class of gift is involved in each of the three stories at the beginning of session 1?**

   The gift of interpretation of tongues—this is a growth gift.

4. **List two advantages that gifts of the growth class might have over gifts of the other classes in illustrating the blessings of the Holy Spirit?**

   a. While primary gifts are more valuable in themselves, growth gifts can have the advantage of being more spectacular and obvious expressions of the Holy Spirit. This can sometimes make a growth gift a more convincing testimony to others that God did indeed intervene. This advantage is partly offset by the danger of attributing divine authorship to purely human thoughts. As we will explore more fully in later sessions, we should be cautious in assuming experiences of this kind are a special communication from God.

 b. In instances where a specific message is involved, growth gifts may reveal inspired ideas more specifically and clearly.

5. Why might we say the primary and skill gifts are "ends in themselves" while the others are not?

A central purpose in life is to develop godly qualities and the talents for effective discipleship. These are qualities we desire in order to live in harmony with God. Therefore when the Holy Spirit strengthens these qualities it is an end in itself.

However, the growth gifts and enabling gifts are specific events which occur to correct a problem or contribute to some godly quality in us. Their purposes relate to those problems or godly qualities. Therefore they are not ends in themselves.

There is danger in cherishing gifts such as prophecy, tongues, and healings as ends in themselves. This is "seeking for signs." As discussed more fully in session 5, it can lead to serious abuse.

6. What might be the logic of listing the gift of healing as both a skill gift and an enabling gift?

Some people have a unique ability to lead others into a healing experience. Others have a special readiness to be healed. These personal qualities are *skill* gifts.

An enabling gift

A specific incident of a healing with the help of the Holy Spirit would be an *enabling* gift.

7. **Rank the three classes according to how strongly the description applies.**

Most closely reflects the nature of God	Most spectacular
a. Primary	a. Enabling
b. Skill	b. Growth
c. Growth	c. Tie—Skill and Primary
d. Enabling	

Primary gifts most closely reflect the nature of God because they are actually qualities of the divine. Skill gifts are next in revealing God's nature. They may reveal a godly quality of leadership or insight on some talent, but will not be as personal a revelation of God. Growth gifts convey specific ideas, but do not represent as much depth of understanding or qualities of God as do the primary gifts. Enabling gifts tend to be physical occurrences from which we may draw useful lessons, but in themselves may not convey much godly thought.

Enabling gifts are the most spectacular. They offer physical evidence of God at work. Growth gifts are the next most spectacular because they are specific, articulate messages. The primary and skill gifts, which are the most fundamental and usually the most important, are the least spectacular. This is because they involve internal qualities rather than observable events.

8. **In each of the four classes, describe one experience in which a gift was received. Evaluate each experience to determine which type of gift it was.**

One experience from the group for each class of

gift should be sufficient unless there is more time left. It might help to arrange in advance for students or others to present these experiences.

9. **What are some reasons for wanting gifts of each class?**
   Primary gifts help us
   • develop broad and deep understanding,
   • become a whole and happy person,
   • get along better with others,
   • become a wiser and more beneficial influence to others,
   • commune better with God.
   Skill gifts help us
   • be a more fruitful disciple of Christ,
   • be more helpful to family and friends,
   • find greater satisfaction in activities.
   Growth gifts help us
   • develop a specific insight,
   • show God's presence,
   • solve a problem.
   Enabling gifts help us
   • solve a problem,
   • cure an illness,
   • show God's presence,
   • demonstrate God's love.

10. **What are some dangers of seeking growth or enabling gifts without having the primary gifts firmly in control of the experience?**
    This is dealt with more fully in session 5. At this time all that is needed is for us to recognize that some people have a difficult time distinguishing an emotional experience from a spiritual experience. They can then use an emotional experience to justi-

fy some ungodly conclusions, if primary gifts such as wisdom, knowledge, faith, discernment, love, and kindness do not dominate the experience.

11. **How would the teaching of Doctrine and Covenants 85:2 and 3 that God is involved in all things affect one's attitude toward the following situations?**
In all five situations explore which of these attitudes might apply.
- In the midst of any danger, God is available to give courage.
- No matter how painful the trial, God is available to give strength.
- In the deepest secrets of our hearts, God understands and our private decisions make a difference.
- In the most difficult tasks, God is there, ready, even anxious to help.
- In every decision, God can help us clarify the issues and cultivate the big perspective.

12. **How does it affect prayer to realize we are not inviting God to come, but are trying to open our eyes to the God who is already there?**
We discover the key function of prayer is not to motivate God to come, but rather to prepare ourselves to receive. Discuss what attitudes we should strive to develop in this preparation. Possibilities are tolerance, understanding, open seeking for truth, love, concern for others, confidence God will respond, commitment to justice, and a strong sense of stewardship. As we struggle to open our minds to the larger understandings of God in these areas, blessings can occur.

A DEPENDABLE GOD

KEY CONCEPT: Spiritual Principles

KEY STATEMENT: Spiritual experience occurs when our partnership with God becomes visible to us.

OBJECTIVES

At the end of the session you should be able to
1. explain four principles of spirituality;
2. recall incidents which illustrate each principle;
3. describe how the fruits of the spirit can enrich our lives.

Humility is required in dealing with the things of God. Full understanding is beyond our human minds. We live with the knowledge that our best understanding today will someday be replaced by another insight and that still will not be all.

Yet, the acts of God are not chaotic. Spiritual gifts are not capricious; they are purposeful. Over the ages God consistently shows certain qualities and observes certain principles. From this experience we can draw helpful guidelines.

Here are four guidelines that may help us deal with spiritual gifts with more insight.

THE PRINCIPLE OF NEED

If we would develop a mature spirituality, we must first understand the principle of need.

President F. Henry Edwards once said, "need is the first law of spirituality."

When I went to my first Melchisedec priesthood retreat, the oldest man in camp was Oscar Case, then in his nineties. Two of us visited with him about his experiences. We asked Oscar if there was any one spiritual gift that he had been blessed with more than others. He said something like,

Yes, dreams. Even as a young man when the Lord had something to tell me, he would usually tell it through a dream. This is unusual because most people don't cultivate the gift of dreams until later in life. I had so many marvelous experiences with these spiritual dreams that I came to expect it, but I never had the gift of tongues. It seemed to me it would be the most marvelous experience if I could have such a spectacular gift as tongues. So I prayed about it a number of times. Finally, I had another dream. The Lord said to me, "Oscar, you need a lot of things worse than the gifts of tongues. Forget it!"

Now there is a wide range of circumstances in which blessings can occur. However, one of the consistent pat-

*Oscar
Case
preach-
ing at
100
years*

terns is that there will be a real need which should not
be met in some other way.

*Q 1 Share an experience in which God responded to
meet a real need. Many testimonies concern
physical healing or other spectacular blessings, so
try to balance the picture here with the equally important but quieter blessings such as we experience
in everyday life. Share experiences such as
    when I needed insight and got it,
    when I needed courage and got it,
    when I had a tough decision and was guided,
    when I needed peace of mind and got it.*

THE PRINCIPLE OF THE BY-PRODUCT

\#   I once taught a Doctrine and Covenants class for
two years. I analyzed each lesson the best I could. I felt

equal to the task; I grew some and helped the class grow. I had the satisfaction of doing a worthwhile thing. But I had no spiritual experience of consequence. About that same period I was to lead a discussion on Zion at a young adult retreat at Camp Doniphan. I felt a strong need to dig deeper than ever before on this subject. Many of us there needed a deeper and clearer understanding than we had. I worked hard but didn't feel anything I read or could offer was good enough. After supper, just before the discussion, I rowed across the lake to be alone in one last effort to think things through more clearly. While floating near an old tree stump, I looked at the minnows swimming around the oar as it bobbed up and down in the waves. I asked, "How will Zion be any different for those minnows from the life they now know?"

I wasn't praying. I was struggling. Then the answers started flooding upon me with a clarity and an insight that was more than my own. The Holy Strengthener met my need.

\# Charles Graham taught that finding spirituality is like finding true happiness. We usually don't get it by seeking it directly. We usually find spirituality by investing ourselves in good works that require more than our best. When we have done our best, God may push us beyond. We then find our spiritual testimony as a by-product of facing the challenge of a church school class, a pastorate, a scout troop, a choir, a college degree, a personality problem, helping our child or friend mature.

It seems to work like this. What we can do, we do alone, no matter how worthy the cause.

But when, in confronting the problems of life or in the service of the Lord, we undertake more than we are capable of, something remarkable can happen. We meet the conditions of this special formula. When we have

Charles
V.
Graham

invested all that we are and have in a good cause, and more is needed, we may feel a steadying hand on our shoulder and that more is supplied. Then we are aware that God is there. We are God's partner.

Q 2 *Describe a personal experience which met the conditions of the "special formula" and where God helped.*

THE PRINCIPLE OF ADVENTURE

Just carrying a heavy load does not encourage a spiritual experience. If after performing excess drudgery we take on more, we may develop ulcers. We may become frustrated and short-tempered. But that alone does not qualify us for a blessing.

If we are struggling for ways to do things better, get

others properly involved, find meaning and purpose in it, or grow in the experience, and we petition God to help us grow, we may find the divine strength added to ours.

Spirtuality exists at the growing edge. If there is an eternal dimension to our task, and we are breaking new ground on which we need growth or healing, and we are open to the inflow of the Spirit, extraordinary things may happen.

Q 3 In the stories about teaching a class and leading a discussion at Camp Doniphan, how does the principle of adventure apply to one and not the other?

Q 4 Why was it reasonable for one experience to receive an obvious blessing and not the other?

THE PRINCIPLE OF GOOD FRUIT

Now the works of the flesh are manifest, which are these, adultery, fornication, uncleanness, lasciviousness, idolatry, witchcraft, hatred, variance, emulations, wrath, strife, seditions, heresies, envyings, murders, drunkenness, revellings, and such like; of the which I tell you before, as I have also told you in time past, that they which do such things shall not inherit the kingdom of God. But the fruit of the Spirit is love, joy, peace, long-suffering, gentleness, goodness, faith, meekness, temperance; against such there is no law.—Galatians 5:19-23 IV

If the great love and broad perspective of God is present in an experience, it will trigger our love and nobility. If an experience generates strife, hatred, envy, immorality, or pettiness it did not come from the Holy Spirit. The Holy Spirit can come into a situation where these human failings are present, but the fruit of the Spirit is always to call us above them.

Q 5 Describe incidents in which you or another person felt led to take a harsh, judgmental position; or to act unkindly; or to violate any fruit of the Spirit

46

listed in Galatians. What were the consequences of the action or attitude?

Q 6 What might have been the results if the person had felt led to exhibit one of the fruits of the Spirit?

This principle of good fruit is so important that it is developed more fully in session 5.

KEY INSIGHTS

While spirituality is beyond our full understanding, there are some helpful guidelines which help us deal with it more effectively.

True spirituality comes, often unexpectedly, as we struggle to meet needs at the growing edge of our experience.

There is an underlying theme to spiritual gifts. Here is the heart of it:

Each of us is called to be co-creator with God of a better life within, a better world round about.

Spiritual experience is an event in which this partnership with God becomes evident. The degree of my spirituality depends largely on the maturity of the partnership I have formed with God.

A strength of the Restoration church is our emphasis on this feeling of partnership.

A true spiritual experience can be identified by its fruit: love, joy, peace, long-suffering, gentleness, goodness, faith, meekness, temperance.

DISCUSSION COMMENTS

1. **Share an experience in which God responded to meet a real need.** So many testimonies concern physical healing or other spectacular blessings, we want to balance the picture here with the equally important but quieter blessings such as we experience in everyday life. Share experiences such as

   when I needed insight and got it,
   when I needed courage and got it,
   when I had a tough decision and was guided,
   when I needed peace of mind and got it.

   The teacher should have a story from personal experience. Use it to trigger a response from one or two members of the class. It might stimulate ideas to list the kinds of need that the Spirit responds to in our everyday lives.

2. **Describe a personal experience which met the conditions of the "special formula" and where God helped.**

   Once again, the teacher may have to offer some ideas to trigger the thinking of others.

3. **In the stories about teaching a class and leading a discussion at Camp Doniphan, how does the principle of adventure apply to one and not the other?**

   When teaching the Doctrine and Covenants class, I was operating well within my capabilities. I was not striving to do more than I was able to do easily. There was little spirit of adventure. However, at Camp Doniphan I was plunging in over my depth. I was dissatisfied with my best and was struggling for something much more.

4. **Why was it reasonable for one experience to receive an obvious blessing and not the other?**

In the Doctrine and Covenants class I was not asking for a blessing, and I was not putting myself in a position where one was needed. It is unlikely for a casual service to lead to a spiritual blessing, however beneficial and noble the service might be.

At Camp Doniphan I was not consciously asking for a blessing. Instead, I was struggling beyond the limits of my capabilities in a good cause and I certainly needed a blessing. I met the requirements of the first three principles of spirituality which were listed in this session.

5. **Describe incidents in which you or another person felt led to take a harsh, judgmental position; or to act unkindly; or to violate any fruit of the Spirit listed in Galatians. What were the consequences of the action or attitude?**

It might help start the discussion to suggest types of stories; the father who moved ruthlessly to stop a marriage of his daughter because he did not want it; the student who developed hostility toward a teacher who had disciplined firmly; the woman who developed a destructive envy toward another who could afford better things; the businessman who accused his rival of dishonest tactics without solid evidence.

6. **What might have been the results if the person had felt led to exhibit one of the fruits of the Spirit?**

This is another case where there is no one right answer. With some sensitivity to the issues involved, anyone should be able to name several good possibilities on each story. Consider the possibilities in several areas such as beneficial effects on the person who had received the harshness, how it might benefit the person who had performed the harshness, how society or the organization might have been helped. We cannot know what would have happened, but these reasonable alternatives tell a great deal about the ways spirituality can enrich our lives. They also alert us to ways of judging if it was genuinely the Holy Spirit.

BEYOND WORDS, BEYOND MEANING

SESSION 4

KEY CONCEPT: Finite Perception

KEY STATEMENT: We see the unlimited light of God through the small windows of the human mind.

OBJECTIVES

At the end of the session you should be able to

1. list reasons for the great contrast between the full vision God could share and the limited fraction we can report;
2. explain the need for continuing prophecy and an open canon of scripture;
3. explain why the church does not teach plenary revelation.

In every experience involving you and me there is always the human element. Most of the time our experiences seem totally human.

Sometimes we are conscious that something more than human is involved... just a vague suggestion.

Sometimes this element becomes so specific we can tell it is the divine.

Sometimes the divine dominates the experience. Yet the essence of the experience is the divine quickening of the human. The human personality is a filter which limits and colors what is understood.

HUMAN

HUMAN

HUMAN

DIVINE

HUMAN

DIVINE

Of course these two interact with each other and the environment in wonderfully complex ways. However, for our present purpose, let us focus on the reaction of the human mind to a divine stimulus.

When I was a boy we held prayer meetings in the neighbors' backyards during the summertime. No one had air conditioning. One Wednesday night we were meeting with Leonard Lea, then editor of the *Saints' Herald*. As Leonard sat before his neighbors conducting the service, the Spirit moved him very strongly. He was given a vision of the potential for outstanding achievement, for nobility of soul, of which each of us was capable. He was given a crushing sense of the awful disparity between the excellence which God hoped for us

and the mediocrity to which most of us had limited ourselves.

Under the influence of the Spirit, Leonard challenged us to see the excellence of which we were capable and which God desired for us. The Spirit moved Leonard with such power that he spoke with more emotion than I had ever seen in him. Normally, he was a restrained intellectual. I was only about twelve years old at the time, but I remember it clearly.

After the service I overheard him discuss it with some of the adults. He sensed that in spite of his best efforts, he was able to grasp only a portion of what God had to say about us—and he realized that his words conveyed even less to us of the deep insights that he felt.

Q 1 In the following analysis, discuss to what part of the Leonard Lea story each step applies.

\# This helps illustrate the problem Leonard Lea was explaining. This problem has confronted every prophet. In life's experiences, the mind of God contains unlimited truth, undistorted by our bias.

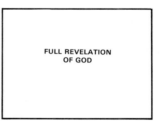

\# When we are open to the limitless mind of God, our human filters limit and color the wisdom and feeling that are there. A gifted prophet may be open to God more fully than most of us with all our fears and prejudices. But the greatest of prophets in the

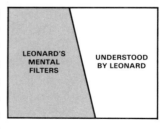

finest of moments compre-
hends but a fragment of the
event.

And what we *do* sense of
God's influence, we can only
partly put into words for
others.

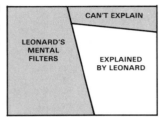

When a second person
tries to understand a spiritual
experience reported by another, the experience is filtered
through the second person's
cultural conditioning. These
influences include a personal
view of how the world functions, self-conscious image,
and ability to reason.

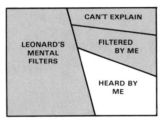

Since the reader experi-
ences only what is written
here, even less communication
occurs. You will not receive
the feeling Leonard communi-
cated when the group heard
him speak. If you were of a
different culture these words
would convey even less.

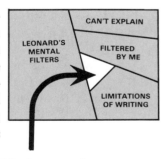

**All that readers
receive of the great
truths God shares.**

This problem is inherent in God's dealing with finite minds such as ours.

Q 2   What reason does the above analysis suggest to support these ideas?
  a.   We need continuing prophetic leadership.
  b.   Scripture is a mixture of human and divine elements.
  c.   We need an open canon of scripture.
  d.   We can never rest on the assumption that we already have the fullness of the gospel.
  e.   We must always be engaged in the exciting adventure of growing with God.

\#   **HOW DOES REVELATION WORK?**

Joseph Smith III accepted leadership of the Reorganization when he was twenty-seven years old.

He saw others lead people astray with mistaken notions. He feared that because of his inexperience he too might not be sure which of his thoughts were enlightened by God and which were not. He could then fall into the same trap of leading people astray.

He assumed spiritual giants had some kind of a special spiritual key that enabled them to say, "This is of Joseph but that is of God." He earnestly desired such a key so he could be a sure prophet.

Over the years he discovered there is no special key. Instead, in a lifetime of experience Joseph Smith III discovered when and how God moves within life. He grew to discern divine wisdom in an action or an idea with greater assurance, frequency, and accuracy. Joseph could then more confidently say if something were "of God."

At the beginning of his presidency, Joseph III provided effective leadership and did much writing for the church. Yet he went so many years at a time without an inspired document that he was criticized as the "silent prophet." As his experience with God grew in later years, he provided numerous inspired documents which are cherished by the church.

Q 3   a. *In light of the previous reading what does the term "silent prophet" indicate about Joseph III?*

b. *What does Joseph's experience indicate about the importance of preparation to being prophetic?*

The most authoritative statement on how Joseph Smith, Jr., translated the Book of Mormon is reported in Section 9 of the Doctrine and Covenants.

Oliver Cowdery was transcribing as Joseph Smith dictated. Oliver thought it would be a thrill if he could

*Oliver
Cowdery*

translate like Joseph. He requested the opportunity several times. Finally permission was given. A hopeful but fearful Oliver waited for the Lord to fill his mind. Nothing happened. A crestfallen Oliver was spoken to in Section 9 with these words:

> Behold, you have not understood; you have supposed that I would give it unto you, when you took no thought, save it was to ask me; but, behold, I say unto you, that you must study it out in your mind; then you must ask me if it be right, and if it is right, I will cause that your bosom shall burn within you; therefore, you shall feel that it is right; but if it be not right, you shall have no such feelings, but you shall have a stupor of thought, that shall cause you to forget the thing which is wrong; therefore, you cannot write that which is sacred, save it be given you from me.—Doctrine and Covenants 9:3

Q 4   *Recall the principles of spirituality in session 3. In what ways is Section 9 consistent with them?*

Q 5   *Why is it important for the person receiving revelation to make so much effort?*

Q 6   *The Apostle Paul wrote, "The spirits of the prophets are subject to the prophets" (I Corinthians 14:32 IV). What may Paul be saying about the nature of revelation?*

\#   Many Christians believe in plenary inspiration. Plenary means complete, full, absolute, unqualified. In plenary inspiration the thought of God would be fully and accurately impressed in the prophet's mind. What the prophet said would then be the actual words of God. In the early years this view was widely held by many church members, and still is believed by some.

As the Saints have gained experience with the prophetic function, members and leaders alike have discovered that the Holy Spirit does not bypass the human mind. It informs and ennobles our minds in remarkable ways, but the prophet, with human limitations, interprets and expresses a personal understanding.

President
Joseph
Smith III

Joseph Smith III strongly reinforced this principle during his testimony in the Temple Lot Suit in 1893.

We do not consider it [the Inspired Translation by Joseph Smith, Jr.] infallible, nor do we consider the Bible infallible. We do not consider anything that passes through human hands to be infallible. We do not believe in the plenary inspiration of the Bible, and therefore we do not believe it to be infallible. . . . That is [also] our view regarding the Book of Doctrine and Covenants.—From transcript of the Temple Lot Case before the Circuit Court of the United States, Western District of Missouri, Western Division, at Kansas City, 1893, page 493

Q 7 *How is this teaching of Joseph III supported by*
  a. *the explanation of the human element found at the start of this session?*
  b. *the Leonard Lea story?*
  c. *Section 9:3 of the Doctrine and Covenants?*
  d. *I Corinthians 14:32?*

Q 8 *How might we reconcile this view of revelation with experiences where persons feel God gave them specific words?*

TO WHAT DOES THE SPIRIT WITNESS?

To What Does the Spirit Witness?

In the early years of his ministry, Bishop John Gorker had an experience which helped him appreciate the human limitations involved in interpreting a spiritual experience. Bishop Gorker explains it this way:

In the first years of my ministry I had strong convictions about the literal truth of everything in scripture. I preached enthusiastically about such things as the symbols of the monsters in the Book of Revelation. I felt the warm reassurance of the Spirit in those sermons and felt the desire to learn more about these ideas. As I studied I discovered some problems with my previous understanding. However, I remembered the reassurance of the Spirit which I had felt when I preached these things, so I continued preaching them. I felt empty; the old warm glow was gone.

I repeated this attempt to preach the old ideas at a reunion I shared with President F. Henry Edwards. I had the same empty feeling. I asked President Edwards, "What is wrong? I know these ideas are true because the Holy Spirit rested on me so strongly when

John Gorker

I preached them in the past. I'm trying as hard now as then. Why do I feel so empty when I say these things now?"

President Edwards replied, "The Holy Spirit was not assuring you those things were true." I was so startled I nearly fell over.

President Edwards explained something like this: "The Holy Spirit does not testify of truth. If it did it would never speak. Human understanding is always imperfect. The Holy Spirit can only assure us that in our imperfect way we are on the right track or the wrong track, and nudge us to move in the direction we should go. At the beginning of your ministry your ideas probably ranged from excellent to erroneous. But you were doing the best you could with what you had. You needed assurance you were doing a good thing and should continue. You got it. You also were urged to study and grow in this area. You did. Now you have the insight which should enable you to preach with more adequate understanding than you were capable of then. As long as you repeat ideas you should have grown beyond, you are not doing your best and you should not expect the Spirit to continue to reassure you."

Q 9   *Relate an experience in which you or another person felt spiritual reassurance, yet with the wisdom of hindsight, you can see that some of the views expressed were imperfect. In that experience, what was the Spirit affirming? What was it not affirming?*

Q 10   *What is a possible problem in recognizing that the Spirit may be supporting the person in an experience without agreeing with all that is said?*

Q 11   *How does this relate to the need for continuing revelation and an open canon of scripture?*

Q 12   *How does this relate to the teaching of Joseph Smith III that the church does not believe in plenary inspiration?*

KEY INSIGHTS

While inspiration can bring great truths to us, our understanding and telling of it is always a human attempt that falls short.

Even prophets suffer this human limitation. At its best, scripture contains only partial statements about adventures with God.

This makes the Restoration principles of continued prophetic leadership and open canon of scripture priceless assets in our effectiveness as a church and our personal growth toward godly understanding.

DISCUSSION COMMENTS

1. **In the following analysis, discuss to what part of the Leonard Lea story each step applies.**

   The first box represents the full truth people might have if there were no human limitations involved.

   The second box shows the human mental filters which Leonard acknowledged when he sensed that in spite of his best efforts, he was able to grasp only a portion of what God had to say about us.

   The third box illustrates how he realized that none of his words conveyed to us more than a fraction of the great insights that he felt.

   Box four illustrates my limitations as a young boy trying to grasp what Leonard Lea had said.

My description of the visual impression that
Leonard made on me, and my reference to the fact
that I remember it clearly, although I was only
twelve years old at the time, refer to insights I had
that I cannot put on paper and convey to a reader,
box five.

2. **What reasons does the above analysis suggest
   to support these ideas?**
   a. **We need continuing prophetic leadership.**
   b. **Scripture is a mixture of human and divine
      elements.**
   c. **We need an open canon of scripture.**
   d. **We can never rest on the assumption that
      we already have the fullness of the gospel.**
   e. **We must always be engaged in the exciting
      adventure of growing with God.**

The answers on all five are much the same. We
need to be open to continued growth and insight
partly because in each age Christianity has new
problems to confront on which help is needed. We
have new insights which need to be interpreted. In
addition, the central message of this session is that
records of God's activity in the past contain inadequate images of what actually transpired. Even
scripture is subject to the limitations we have been
talking about. The best of the prophets understood
but a fragment of what God had to share. Those
who heard the prophets speak were able to grasp
only part of what was being said. Those who later
wrote the record down could capture only a portion
of what the eyewitnesses saw and felt. For this
reason, it is an impoverished religion that relies
entirely on the record of the past. All of humanity

has a great need for continuing revelation to supplement the past record.

3. a. **In light of the previous reading what does the term "silent prophet" indicate about Joseph III?**

It suggests Joseph was a man of integrity. He was careful not to credit the inspiration for an idea to God until he was sure. It suggests he may have had the dedication and courage to move ahead in faith to assume the responsibility of prophet even though he felt his humanity limited him from being fully prepared to function as one.

   b. **What does Joseph's experience indicate about the importance of preparation to being prophetic?**

Functioning prophetically is more than a matter of being ordained to an office. It requires study, faith, and confidence to move out. The prophetic role involves wisdom and practiced skill in discerning the mind of God. These qualities grow with experience.

4. **Recall the principles of spirituality in session 3. In what ways is Section 9 consistent with them?**

The method described in Section 9 of the Doctrine and Covenants meets the principle of need. The spokesman is struggling for insight to accomplish an important purpose. It satisfies the requirements of the principle of the by-product because the spokesman is struggling to accomplish his task; he is not seeking a sign. It satisfies the principle of adventure because he is pushing beyond the limits of his understanding and breaking unfamiliar ground.

5. **Why is it important for the persons receiving a revelation to make so much effort?**

Spiritual power augments our power. The more intensely our powers are mobilized, the more laudable the resulting service can be. Also, unless we have pushed ourselves to our limit, we have not satisfied the requirements of the principle of need or the principle of adventure.

6. **The Apostle Paul wrote, "The spirits of the prophets are subject to the prophets." What may Paul be saying about the nature of revelation?**

Paul was saying that the prophet is responsible for his inspired thinking and the use he makes of it. He was acknowledging the element of human stewardship in every spiritual experience.

7. **How is this teaching of Joseph III supported by**
   a. The explanation of the human element found at the start of this session?

   In every prophetic experience, the prophet is interpreting what happens and the resulting message is limited and colored by personal attitudes, expressions, and limitations.

   b. The Leonard Lea story?

   While the prophet reports the experience as accurately as possible, because of human filters he brings us only a portion of what God makes available.

c. Section 9:3 of the Doctrine and Covenants?

The prophet has to make a significant investment in what happens. God gives an assurance of the rightness of what is said, or may warn of error. The Spirit may support, clarify, and enrich. There is a great deal of the prophet as well as of God in any prophetic utterance.

d. I Corinthians 14:32?

The human limitation of the prophet can limit the message of the Spirit.

8. How might we reconcile this view of revelation with experiences where persons feel God gave them specific words?

The important truth here is that God does not use prophets the way an author uses a typewriter. As this sentence is dictated the machine faithfully reproduces what is said and you will read exactly the words intended. God does not use people as typewriters. God may quicken us or direct us, but we remain active agents whenever we function as messengers. The message always bears our imprint. Sometimes the Spirit merely gives a slight nudge. Other times we have the feeling of being strongly directed. There may be a few cases where it appears that a particular phrase should be used. However, even when the prophet indicates that God is speaking, the vocabulary, faith assumptions, and outlook of the prophet usually color the message. Generally the prophets struggle in their own words to express the insights they feel are approved by the Holy Spirit.

9. **Relate an experience in which you or another person felt spiritual reassurance, yet, with the wisdom of hindsight, you can see that some of the views expressed were imperfect. In that experience, what was the Spirit affirming?**

From what we know of God, we can be confident that the Spirit would not affirm error or immature understanding. Look for the strengths which were needed and given, or the new understanding which came at that time and has stood the test of time.

What was it not affirming?

Probably any parts of the experience which look doubtful to you today are preconceptions the person brought to the experience, or feelings which arose from the person's own preconceptions.

10. **What is a possible problem in recognizing that the Spirit may be supporting the person in an experience without agreeing with all that is said?**

This may mean that the person will not be sure what is meant until the wisdom of hindsight comes, months or years later. It may lead to reluctance to ever believe that God is involved in an experience.

11. **How does this relate to the need for continuing revelation and an open canon of scripture?**

This says the Holy Spirit may lead people to understandings beyond their time in one area, but not lead them consciously from cherished views they are not ready to give up, nor lead them to new views they are not ready to accept. Thus, Joseph Smith, Jr., frequently delivered instruction which revealed a deeper and more accurate understanding than he had two years before on such subjects as stewardship and Zion. The finest of the prophets in the finest of their moments were partly prisoners of their time, culture, and personal biases. They were capable of only a partial understanding. Revelation and scripture are helpful, but not final. On every subject more light is possible, and needed.

12. How does this relate to the statement of Joseph Smith III that the church does not teach plenary inspiration?

This is an application of that teaching. Joseph said that everything that passes through human hands is defective because God merely quickens the human mind but does not impose absolute truth upon it. F. Henry Edwards was applying the same understanding to the problems of church members who grow beyond where they were when they first sensed the Holy Spirit confirming their efforts.

IS IT REALLY GOD?

SESSION 5

KEY CONCEPT: Spiritual Discernment

KEY STATEMENT: Spirituality is dangerous if we do not discern the human and divine element in every spiritual experience.

OBJECTIVES

At the end of the session you should be able to

1. list five spiritual snares that cause abuse of spiritual gifts;
2. list three results of seeking spectacular gifts excessively;
3. list and apply evidences of true spirituality.

SPIRITUAL SNARES

Like all good things, spiritual gifts can be abused. Their great power and appeal make it tempting to use the gifts improperly. Their thorough mingling of human and godly elements makes delusion easy.

Here are five spiritual snares that lead many astray:

Excitement

When God moves dramatically in our lives, it is pretty heady stuff. Most want more. Particularly if life has been drab or unproductive, there is a natural human tendency to keep chasing the excitement of growth or enabling gifts. Even worse, some go on emotional binges where there is no gift at all.

Escapism

Among a people who are impoverished or oppressed, dramatic spirituality can be an escape from the futility of life. This generally degenerates into emotionalism. This may have some therapeutic value, perhaps superior to reading a detective book, having a drink, or certain other forms of escapism. This emotionalism is a far cry from the ennobling effects of true spirituality.

Abnormal Psychic Needs

Some people have an abnormal need for love, security, or recognition. A few turn compulsively to spiritual manifestations, rather than confront the need realistically.

An acquaintance has an obsessive need to be honored by others. He has found that when he speaks in tongues and utters prophecies and claims to be a spokesman for God, some people are impressed and revere him. This has lured him into leading others into emotional excesses. It has caused him to ignore the gifts of wisdom and discernment which would have saved him and his followers from much mischief.

Pressure from the Congregation

At the conclusion of the first reunion where I was the guest minister, I felt it would be a tremendous experience for the congregation if I could bring them a spiritual message in my final sermon. If it were genuine, I knew it could be a real blessing to many of the people there. I very much wanted it to happen. Several times during that sermon I struggled for assurance that God would approve a sweeping challenge or specific assurance on pressing matters. Instead, every time I found myself pushed toward a statement which could be supported only by common wisdom. Each time it was made very clear to me that if I said any more it was strictly my own speculation. In the years since, I have concluded that that experience probably was the most beneficial one I could have had. We should never try to force the hand of God. We should not even try to anticipate too strongly how God might direct us in a given situation. Our noble and loving desire to minister can sometimes push us too far.

Justification of Personal Desires

When we want something badly enough, it is easy to assume God wants it too. If we want to gain an honor, prove a point of doctrine, buy an expensive car, avoid a responsibility, if we want anything badly, it is easy to puff up the points for it and set aside the points against it. The case for what we want is then so obvious it is all we can hear.

The fire of desire can be interpreted as the fire of the Spirit.

71

Q 1 Describe incidents in which you have seen some of these spiritual snares exhibited. What were the consequences?

RESULTS OF SPIRITUALISTIC ADDICTION

Some people are addicted to spiritual experiences. They seek spiritual signs for their own sake. When any virtue is cherished out of proportion to others, the results are unfortunate. Interestingly, this is as true of spirituality as any other part of life.

Persons who are totally engrossed in weight lifting will have the advantage of great physical strength. But such a narrow focus to their lives may possibly rob them of speed or mental and social development.

Likewise, persons who become seekers after spiritual signs, and who develop an avid taste for spectacular gifts should have some laudable traits, such as deep faith, inner serenity, or effective outreach. However, such a narrow focus can prevent balanced development and leave them vulnerable to several excesses. A study by Donald Comer in one church region where this spiritualism was most evident revealed three consistent problems. He reports the following:

Ignoring of Major Gifts

Some persons are attracted to religious activities where manifestations of the seemingly more spectacular gifts are evident. Occasionally, people have been known to make private collections of "prophecies." Others have the reputation of being devotees of well-known "gift" practitioners. To those so enticed, the major gift areas of wisdom, faith, knowledge, and discernment may seem drab and unsatisfying by comparison. There is abundant evidence that when secondary gift interest becomes dominant and the role of the primary gifts is lessened, stunted spiritual stature results.

Becoming Spiritually Arrogant

There may exist a "having a corner on the truth" enrapturement

*Donald
Comer*

by some who feel they have been especially favored with a spiritual gift. One needs to be reminded of the perils of ego inflation associated with gift manifestation. Any legitimate possession of such gifts as prophecy, miracle-working, or tongues must be accompanied by healthy insights gained from wisdom and knowledge together with a fair measure of humility. If not, there are likely to be forms of arrogance which are detrimental to the spirit of Christ-centeredness.

Leaving the Church

With a growing addiction to the spectacular and an increasing indifference to the less-dramatic gifts, lured persons often flock where the glitter of these attractions are found. Allegiance may shift from the church and its broader concerns to some group which emphasizes a particular gift specialty. Unfortunately, there is a common failure to recognize that spiritual maturity and "gift" manifestation are quite different. Church members who persist in their quest for the most charismatic gifts and signs are often subject to motivations and influences totally unrelated to the church's belief system and practice.

73

Q 2   In addition to presenting the spiritual excesses, list
three reasons for needing to know how to determine
if an experience is genuinely of the Holy Spirit.

a.

_____

b.

_____

c.

_____

EVIDENCES OF TRUE SPIRITUALITY

We have no fixed list to which we can look which will assure us whether or not an experience is validly spiritual. Each situation is unique. Each situation is a complex of many factors. Some factors are difficult to define. This is further complicated by the fact we considered earlier that most situations contain both divine and human elements. However, because this matter is so extremely important, several ministers have made lists of evidences of true spirituality which can help us exercise greater wisdom. The Apostle Paul, Evan Fry, and Apostle Clifford Cole have done helpful work. The four points below have been refined from their lists. If you can answer yes to all four points, the experience is probably divinely inspired. If the answer is no to any point, be very cautious in assuming that it represents the word of God.

In addition to these tests, it is helpful to check if

Apostle
Clifford
Cole

any of the spiritual snares are present or if the
principles of spirituality were in operation. These
may give helpful warnings or assurances.

A. We sense awe.

If God is present in the experience, we will
sense something grander than ourselves. This
can take many forms, depending on our
need. There may be exhilaration, there may
be calm serenity, there may be a limitless
love, there may be a sense of majesty and
power. Not all of these would be present at
any one time, but there will be the sense of
something more than human, if the experience is not purely human.

The sense of awe accentuates our contrasting limitation. This is not a case of self-abasement. There may actually be an exhilarating sense of our tremendous potential. The important thing is that however worthy we find ourselves to be, we feel dwarfed by something greater.

This sense of awe may be so subtle we are not conscious of it until later. For that reason this test is often more helpful in giving confirmation than in giving a sure answer by itself.

B. We crave to respond to God's call.

If God is present in the situation, we are drawn as to a magnet. God's love triggers our love. God's wisdom expands our wisdom. We yearn to immerse ourselves in this great goodness that we feel. We yearn to serve the divine purpose. Our attention is drawn from our own narrow, partisan ambitions.

C. Our total person is quickened.

An encounter with God is an encounter by our total person. The God who exists in total quickens us in total.

If our emotions are deeply stirred but there is no deepening of understanding, no stimulus of new thought, the divine involvement is probably quite low. The experience may be wholesome; it may be beneficial. But its impact is too narrow for God. It is emotional. It is of us.

Likewise, if we have brilliant, intuitive new thoughts, and it is a purely mental exercise, it is something less than God. If God is present, there will be a stirring sense that so much more is possible. There will be a fervent sense of the importance of what is being said. Or there may be heartache that so many fail to see this crucial message. If God is involved, our total being will be quickened. Ideas will be presented with the divine sense of urgency, or appreciation, or motivation, or other emotion in addition to the intellectual content.

D. The message is sound.

God leads us toward wisdom and justice. This does not encourage detours or error.

I heard of a woman who feels that God instructed her to marry a certain man. She was already married to a good man with whom she could have had a good marriage. This instruction to marry the second man was doubtful ethics. We can question whether God had much to do with her feelings.

This may be a dangerous test to apply because frequently God is leading us in unfamiliar paths. It is easy to say, "By my standards this is not right, so it can't be of God." When Joseph Smith taught that the scriptural record was in error at some points, there were those who were scandalized and said, "This cannot be of God."

It is necessary that we maintain an open mind and be prepared for God to lead us to new and unexpected growth. On the other hand, when instruction comes which leads to bigotry, narrowness of viewpoint, immorality, or harshness, *beware.* Instruction that calls us to less than godliness is from a less-than-godly source.

Q 3 *In the following cases mark each passage which contains the following evidences with the letter for that type.*

 a. evidence of spiritual snares

 b. evidence that God was involved

 c. evidence that it was basically a human experience

After marking each story, the class should discuss.

\# My name is Ellen. Last year my life was pretty rough. I got tired of Mom and Dad fighting so much. I didn't like to go home from school. I couldn't see that any of us were headed anywhere.

One time at Mary's house one of the guys got us to try pot. That seemed like a big adventure, and I sure needed one. Pretty soon I was into drugs pretty good. My grades went downhill. I almost flunked courses that would have been easy the year before. I was headed for the pits.

Then I found Jesus. Meg and Judy asked me to go to the Youth Fellowship with them. I found I liked being in a bunch of kids who were trying to make something of themselves. Everyone made me feel like they really wanted me, so I went back.

The third night Jesus spoke to me. He didn't say anything. He just seemed to be beside me loving me. I knew anytime I came to Jesus he would be there and make me feel good. Jesus is my best friend.

Things at home don't bother me as much now and I'm doing great at school.

Two weeks ago Bob asked Hazel to the class picnic instead of me. It almost wiped me out. Just then Mary asked me for the umpteenth time to go on a party with the old gang. It was an all-day rumble at Blue Lake. For the first time since finding Christ, I was tempted.

Luckily, that night was the Youth Fellowship midweek service. I had to go to sort things out. I never prayed so hard for my friend Jesus to sit beside me and love me. He sure did. I felt so good I couldn't hold it. First thing I knew I was on my feet talking in some foreign tongue like I'd seen some others do. I'm not sure what I said but it sure had a great feel because half the kids had tears. They were really thrilled by what I did. Mike said he thought I spoke Tahitian. Emily thought it was from some lost civilization.

I didn't go to Blue Lake.

\#   My brother, Peter, is trying to raise three small children alone. It's rough. It keeps him drained emotionally, financially—every other way. Yet, when our mother was ill, good-hearted Peter showed the rest of us up by doing so much more for her.

Last spring we were stunned by publicity that Peter had embezzled $8,000 from his employer. Peter was one of the last people you would expect that of. The papers ran stories about big hospital bills, an expensive alimony lawsuit, lonely nights stuck with the kids, a good man trapped in a no-win dead end.

It was humiliating. Things like that don't happen in our family. It looked like someone might have to step in and take care of his kids for weeks or years.

Peter had no right to put us in that position. Besides if we sacrificed to help Peter, wouldn't that make it easier for him to stumble again? Yet, he is our brother. We love him.

I prayed very hard. In a dream I was made to understand that if we sacrifice too much to help Peter that would make it easier for him to stumble again. If he went to prison, we might have to provide homes for his children, but that is all. We should maintain our distance from Peter so our innocent families would not be injured by the publicity, the embarrassment, the financial strain.

KEY INSIGHTS

The thorough mingling of the human with the Divine in spiritual experience makes it easy to misread and misuse spiritual experience.

These dangers are especially present if we have strong emotional needs which cause us to seek anxiously.

Excessive dependence on spectacular gifts is a step away from rather than toward effective partnership with God.

Fortunately we can develop wisdom in discerning if God is present in an experience.

1. We sense something far grander than ourselves.
2. We yearn to serve the divine purpose.
3. We are quickened both mentally and emotionally.
4. The message is sound.

DISCUSSION COMMENTS

1. Describe incidents in which you have seen some of these spiritual snares exhibited.

The class should avoid
- discussing persons anyone can identify, unless it is a story about the speaker,
- adopting a superior attitude.

This is an analysis of a problem, not a put-down or embarrassment of a person. It might be a good idea for the teacher and some students to be prepared with a couple of examples where people fell into spiritual snares. This may encourage others to think of some examples from their lives.

What were the consequences?

Some of the typical consequences of snares might include people being led to do cruel things, make unjustified sacrifices, display arrogance, lose faith, make unwise decisions.

2. In addition to preventing the spiritual excesses, list three reasons for needing to know how to determine if an experience is genuinely of the Holy Spirit.

Some reasons for wanting to know if an experience is genuinely of the Holy Spirit might be

Should we heed the advice which is given?

Is a priesthood call genuine?

Is this activity ultimately right?

What confidence should be placed in the person who brought the message?

3. Ellen's Story

a. Evidence of spiritual snares

Here are some spiritual snares in Ellen's story. There could have been escapism because she said she was not headed anywhere, and later she was headed for the pits. Afterwards she was almost wiped out when Bob asked another girl to the picnic. This may have gone so far as to be an abnormal psychic need. Her deep needs may have contributed to her image of "buddy Jesus." The desire for recognition might have been present in her speaking in tongues since she notes that half the kids had tears and were thrilled by what she did.

b. **Evidence that God was involved**

There is some evidence her experience might have been genuinely spiritual on these counts: she craved to respond to God's call; she has a real yearning for Jesus.

It appears her total person was quickened, although it seemed to be more emotional than intellectual.

The message is sound, judging by the results. Things at home did not bother her; she is doing great at school; she did not go to Blue Lake.

c. **Evidence that it was basically a human experience**

There does not seem to be much sense of awe in her vision of her buddy Jesus. It sounds like a comfortable human image, considerably less than a revelation of God. Her strong psychic needs are not in themselves evidence that there was not a genuine spiritual experience, but they do make us cautious. She seemed overly anxious to have some kind of experience. The fact that the impact of her experience was almost entirely emotional also raises a question. The emotional component is especially evident in her experience of speaking in tongues. There was no translation. Neither she nor anyone else knew what had been said. This is unlike a true spiritual experience. In summarizing Ellen's case, God could have been involved in some of the good things that happened in her life. However, the conscious communications she discussed seem to be primarily human and emotional.

Peter's Story
a. **Evidence of spiritual snares**

The spiritual snare this person exhibits most noticeably is justification of personal desires. His controlling desire was to escape the humiliation and possible financial burden he felt Peter had brought on the family. Note the remark, "Peter had no right to put us in that position." This attitude could have prompted the dream.

b. **Evidence that God was involved**

There is no evidence that this experience met any of the four conditions of a true spiritual experience. There is no sense of the awe that would dwarf human condition. There is no craving to respond to God's great love or wisdom. The message does not appear to be sound.

c. **Evidence that it was basically a human experience**

The message caters exclusively to this person's desire to escape responsibility and embarrassment. The loving concern and helpfulness that would be exhibited by a godly brother or sister are missing. It is very doubtful that God had much to do with this experience.

THE SPIRITUAL "HOW TO" BOOK

SESSION 6

KEY CONCEPT: Building Partnership

KEY STATEMENT: Building a healthy spirituality involves building a productive partnership.

OBJECTIVES

At the end of the session you should be able to

1. explain the relationships between everyday work, practical communication, and ecstatic experience in one's relationship with God;
2. explain the importance of the working partnership to the "Last Supper";
3. describe four steps to a healthy spiritual life.

DIAGRAM OF A HEALTHY MARRIAGE

A healthy married life can teach us something vital about a healthy spiritual life.

Both partners may have personal interests in which the other has limited involvement. However, in this analysis we are looking only at their partnership activities together. In a healthy marriage, both partners spend most of this time together working to strengthen the family and its members. There is the house payment to be met, groceries to be bought, rugs to be cleaned, children to be cared for, guests to be entertained. Sometimes it is drudgery. Sometimes there is deep satisfaction in working shoulder-to-shoulder and triumphing over odds. But, however it is done, most of the marriage partnership involves cooperating to accomplish the daily tasks without fanfare or excitement.

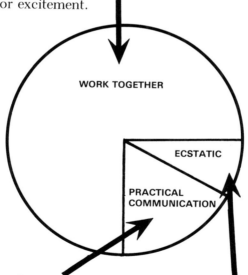

In a healthy marriage, the partners do more than work together.

Occasionally their love must express itself in ecstatic fervor if they are

They also communicate. The tasks are done so much more efficiently if they discuss who should do what and how. The relationship between them is much deeper and more satisfying if they share their triumphs and failures and plan together the future directions of their joint ventures.

to have a really outstanding marriage. These romantic moments are a thing of beauty in themselves. However, this is not their greatest value. The most useful purpose of ecstatic moments in a marriage is to add beauty and commitment to the much larger span of time spent in the work-a-day business of the marriage. At these times, their love is so intense that it colors the relationship at all times. They are able to commit themselves wholeheartedly and permanently to each other. It brings significance to mundane tasks. They find as much joy in bringing happiness to their partners as they could ever find in serving their own projects. All their days are made more serene and happy by the certainty that their partners are equally committed to them.

Q 1 What would happen to a marriage that consisted only of ecstatic moments?

Q 2 In what ways does this balance in a healthy marriage apply to a healthy spirituality?

\# When Christ met with the twelve for the last time, the compelling power and the deep meaning of the Last Supper flowed from three years of active partnership together in history's climactic adventure. Often they had shared a rock for a pillow. They had shared a loaf of bread after many a dusty walk. When the crowds were hostile, they shielded one another. When the crowds were friendly they shared in the adulation. When the Lord fed the five thousand, they were there assisting. Often they marveled at the power of his ministry. They marveled even more that, following his example, they were able to minister likewise. Now the powerful man who stood at the center of this tightly knit fraternity announced that he was to be taken from them. He commanded them to eat the bread and drink the wine in remembrance of him.

So long as these men lived they ate the bread and drank the wine with deep feeling. They drew sustenance from the emblems far beyond the vitamins and calories. It was the stirring renewal of partnership that made it so. So it must be with us.

Q 3 What are the dangers in a spiritual life that is based almost entirely on ecstatic fervor?

Q 4 What are the hazards of a spiritual life that does not include moments of intense feeling?

STEPS TO HEALTHY SPIRITUALITY

Step 1   Line up our purposes with God.

Q 5 In developing a healthy spiritual life, what benefits and limitations would the following actions have?
a. asking the congregation for prayers

b. *asking the pastor what to do*
c. *asking God to give a sign*

   Examples:
   Don't let me become a teacher if I shouldn't.
   Make Herb Jones speak to me during his sermon.
   I'm waiting, tell me what to do.
d. *following the instruction to Oliver Cowdery in Doctrine and Covenants 9:3*

Step 2   Take a responsibility

\# Enter actively into partnership with God. Take a worthy task at hand and do your best. You may or may not have a spiritual experience before entering into such partnership, but enter into partnership anyway.

Q 6 What does the principle of the by-product, session 2, suggest about the importance of this step?

Step 3   Search for the godly dimension in that responsibility

\# We do a good thing when we complete an organization, or handle administrative responsibilities, or plan a fun activity. But we should do more: we should search for ways to help people lead better lives or ways to strengthen God's work. This is the godly dimension.

Q 7 In session 3 contrasting experiences were told on teaching a Doctrine and Covenants class and leading a discussion at Camp Doniphan. What do these say about the importance of this step?

Q 8 Form pairs and discuss with your partner some godly dimensions we might find in
   a. teaching a church school class,
   b. serving on the city council,
   c. being women's commissioner,
   d. working on the yearbook.

Step 4   Make the leap of faith.

\#   Do it. Move out courageously in reliance on God. Our object is to be God's partners.

This is not done by dreaming good deeds or deciding to do good deeds. We must attempt good deeds.

The future may be unsure. We may stumble occasionally; but that is all right. After taking the first three steps, we must plunge ahead.

Repeat step 1 occasionally to be certain about lining up with God. If we are, we are making our best effort at being in partnership with God.

So do it.

And see what God does.

Q 9 In the following cases, describe
   a. how it meets, or fails to meet, each of the spiritual principles in session 3;
   b. how it meets, or fails to meet, the four steps to healthy spirituality in this session;
   c. what some dangers are if the person continues the present course;
   d. what that person should change to improve the chances of a healthy spirituality.

- Henry loves the Bible. He says there is no need for people to be confused. God's great writers have recorded the important truths in scripture. Henry is very impatient with people who fail to read scriptures the way God has commanded. He feels they deserve to stay ignorant.
- Angie joined a charismatic prayer group. She says God speaks to them several times every meeting. God is so loving that if we just open our minds and ask, God will enter in remarkable ways. We will have speaking in tongues, prophecies, healings, and whatever we seek in love and wisdom.

- Max is very efficient. When he became program director of the young adult singles group, he made a chart with a box for every job and he filled all the boxes. Max decided the group mainly wanted to play volleyball, so he organized a volleyball league. Singles never saw such a well-organized league.
- Bertha says God's greatest gift is intelligence. That is what separates people from animals. One of the greatest fulfillments in life comes from studying an important thing until we are an expert in it. If we have a problem, we should not get overly emotional or seek a sign. We must study the problem or consult an expert so we know what to do.

KEY INSIGHTS

A healthy spiritual life requires the balance of working relationship, communication, and intense experience in our partnership with God.

These steps have great value in developing a healthy spirituality:

1. Line up our purposes with God.
2. Take a responsibility in active partnership with God.
3. Search for the godly dimension in that responsibility.
4. Make the leap of faith. (Move out courageously in reliance on God.)

DISCUSSION COMMENTS

1. What would happen to a marriage that consisted only of ecstatic moments?

Such a marriage would lack the physical where-with-all to survive. The bond that comes from building a home, rearing a family, the intimacy of the joint venture would be missing.

The ecstasy of reconciliation cannot be repeated when there is nothing left to reconcile. The ecstasy of fresh commitment cannot be repeated when all commitments are firmly in place. The ecstasy of intimacy cannot be perpetuated when intimacy is over-extended.

Too much repetition transforms fervor to drudgery.

2. In what ways does this balance in a healthy marriage apply to a healthy spirituality?

Everything said about marriage applies here. It is shared experiences, working together, that cement our relationship with God and add meaning to it. And we need to go beyond merely working together. We need a meeting of minds on our purposes and goals. We need communication. Communication arises out of the partnership.

While we should not seek after signs, we should seek communion with God, being open and expectant. From time to time when the need is great, when the time is ripe, our partner will communicate with us in ways that are thrilling and exciting.

This is not just a mystical phenomenon. It will be a natural, cherished part of our work-a-day partnership.

3. **What are the dangers in a spiritual life that is based almost entirely on ecstatic fervor?**

A spiritual life that consists only of ecstatic fervor is shallow. It is as empty as a marriage that consists only of moonlight and roses. Indeed, because true partnership is lacking, it is doubtful that this is true spiritual experience.

4. **What are the hazards of a spiritual life that does not include moments of intense feeling?**

It will be as drab and unstable as a marriage without it. The occasional mountaintop experience with God
- gives our mission purpose,
- helps us find answers to our big questions,
- points us in the right direction,
- gives bounce to our step
- makes life seem worthwhile and precious.

A healthy spirituality is a balanced, positive relationship with a partner.

5. **In developing a healthy spiritual life, what benefits and limitations would the following actions have?**
a. Asking the congregation for prayers
Benefits
- There is often power in the united prayer of the people.
- It can get others involved in supporting our effort and in thinking of ways they might help us.

Limitations
- Seeking the help of others might divert us from the fact that building a good spiritual life is something extremely personal that ultimately we must work out with God.

- Asking the congregation to pray for our blessings may foster the idea that it is something God does to us and that we passively receive, rather than something that is the by-product of our efforts to work with God.

b. Asking the pastor what to do

Benefit

- Another person who is knowledgeable and experienced can frequently see things in our lives that need changing or provide helpful insights on how to proceed.

Limitation

- The pastor cannot really do it for us. Another person can only provide counsel on how we might work it out.

c. Asking God to give a sign

Benefit

- On rare occasions spiritually immature persons may need a sign to strengthen their hopes.

Limitation

- This can foster the idea that spiritual experience is something we passively receive, or something that is unrelated to our active partnership with God. There is real danger in this. The only time this is ever in accord with the principle of need, the principle of the by-product, and the principle of adventure, is when a person is struggling for a most elementary assurance that there is a God who can work in these ways. Even in these limited cases, asking for signs is usually not the best way.

d. Following the instruction to Oliver Cowdery in Doctrine and Covenants 9:3

Benefit

- When we act in this way we are implementing the principles of partnership with God. We will be employing the principles of spirituality discussed previously. This provides the best chance of obtaining beneficial results.

Limitation

- Sometimes no direct blessing is forthcoming even though the person feels a great need. However, this normally indicates that a conspicuous spiritual blessing is not needed at that time, or that the blessing being received is simply not recognized. Actually, this is not a limitation. Any effort to push beyond Doctrine and Covenants 9:3 and force a spiritual blessing is to be avoided. This is seeking after gifts rather than an act of partnership with God.

6. **What does the principle of the by-product, session 3, suggest about the importance of this step?**

   This step is at the heart of the principle of the by-product. True spirituality usually comes as a by-product of our effort to overcome a problem or render a godly service when the challenge is too big for us to handle alone.

7. **In session 3 contrasting experiences were told on teaching a Doctrine and Covenants class and leading a discussion at Camp Doniphan. What do these say about the importance of this step?**

   When teaching the Doctrine and Covenants class, I was not searching for the eternal dimension. I was trying to do a good work, but was content to meet the rather ordinary needs of the class for information. However, when I was to lead the discussion at

Camp Doniphan I was afire with the great potentials and needs of the others. I opened my mind to God. Then I was made to see the increased promise of ministry which those people could give in future years if the right ministry were provided on that occasion. I was stretched beyond my limits by a recognition of the tremendous stakes and the eternal dimension in that responsibility.

This is a reminder that any responsibility can be a rather commonplace task if we are content to merely perform the duties. It is also a reminder that any service to others can be a rewarding partnership with God if we open our minds to God and search for the great human needs to be met and the potentials to be served.

8. **Form pairs and discuss with your partner some godly dimensions we might find in**
   a. **Teaching a church school class**
      - students whose lives are at a crossroads who may become anything from pillars of society to hoodlums
      - students who lack a stable home life and desperately need the love of a mature and godly person
      - students who are lonely and badly need Christian fellowship
      - students who are confused about God and urgently need a mature faith
      - students who have potential for outstanding lives if their faith and skills are nurtured
      - the teacher's own need for theological growth
      - a personal opportunity to develop skills in leadership or in relating to other people
   b. **Serving on the city council**

- political campaign ethics which need to be up-graded
- pressure groups which should be blocked from buying influence
- youths who need recreation facilities and protection from drug dealers
- older persons who need special services
- a community which needs the example of wholesomeness in its leaders

c. **Being Women's Commissioner**
- members who have family trouble and who urgently need a support group
- lonely acquaintances who desperately need to belong to a warm circle of friends
- members who are hooked on bad habits and need moral support to help overcome them
- participants who have leadership talent to be cultivated
- participants who have a desire for Christian service and need an outlet
- members who are confused about their beliefs
- the commissioner's own potential for leadership.
- the commissioner's own need to find meaning in a valuable service

d. **Working on the yearbook**
- people who need to have their self-image reinforced
- co-workers who need the experience of teamwork
- a group that needs to have its good qualities emphasized
- a group that needs an optimistic, constructive, wholesome influence

- a group that needs to develop a feeling of belonging and unity

9. **Henry's Story**
   a. **Describe how it meets, or fails to meet, each of the spiritual principles in session 3.**

   Henry may meet the principle of adventure when he finds challenging new theological concepts in his study. He is content with a surface understanding of what he reads so it is unlikely he meets the principle of need. He does not relate to the principle of the by-product in any significant way. His intolerance of others shows he fails on the principle of good fruit. He will meet all of these principles in a smaller degree than if he were implementing his discipleship in a more active way in meeting the needs of others or of his congregation.

   b. **Describe how it meets, or fails to meet, the four steps to healthy spirituality in this session.**

   If Henry goes no further than is reported here, he will have very little opportunity to fulfill the four steps to a healthy spirituality.

   c. **Describe what some dangers are if the person continues the present course.**

   If Henry continues his present course, it will become increasingly difficult for him to find new adventures with God or needs where God can help him grow. The longer he keeps a narrow focus on the reading of scripture, the more he will become a student of scripture and the less he will become a partner with God.

   d. **Describe what that person should change to improve the chances of a healthy spirituality.**

Henry's greatest need is to involve himself in active discipleship. As he struggles to make good things happen in the world, the things he has studied will take on greater meaning and he will be challenged to new growth opportunities. Henry would also benefit from study of other good books which contain valuable insights beyond those contained in scripture. Even the scriptures will take on much greater meaning for him as he understands the history of the Bible times more accurately, understands better how this universe functions, and is more aware of the needs and opportunities of today.

Angie's Story
a. Describe how it meets, or fails to meet, each of the spiritual principles in session 3.

The kind of charismatic experience Angie is describing may occasionally meet a need. However, with most people it becomes a repetitive experience which they seek regardless of need. Since they are directly seeking spiritual gifts for their own sake, it violates the principle of the by-product. Because they are repeatedly going back to the same source for the same kind of experience, it violates the principle of adventure. The fruits are not known.

b. Describe how it meets, or fails to meet, the four steps to healthy spirituality in this session.

There may be some tendency here for Angie to line herself up with God. However, this seems to be done in a basically emotional and superficial fashion. Beyond seeking a spiritual experience, there does not seem to be much tendency to take on a partnership responsibility. The leap of faith seems to be limited to cultivating spiritual signs. There is no indication of a leap of faith in moving ahead in other parts of her discipleship.

c. **Describe what some dangers are if the person continues the present course.**

If Angie continues in the very narrow and specialized spiritual life, she can expect to become increasingly dependent on spectacular emotional experience. She will become increasingly uncomfortable with people who seek a broader and more productive discipleship. In time she may even become condescending toward those who do not share her "great truth."

d. **Describe what that person should change to improve the chances of a healthy spirituality.**

Angie needs to do two things:

• Develop a broader discipleship by assuming responsibilities in other areas of life in which she can serve Christian purposes. Fortunately, some charismatic people do this and it helps them very much. Unfortunately it does not appear Angie did.

• Angie needs to learn to do good works, and let God decide when and how to move in her life. She will probably have fewer emotional highs, but more substantial encounters with God. These will strengthen her as a person to meet all of life.

Max's Story

a. **Describe how it meets, or fails to meet, each of the spiritual principles in session 3.**

Max meets the law of need to some extent. However, he seems content to focus on one interest and not explore the other important needs in his group. Therefore, he is not confronting some urgent challenges on which he should need spiritual help.

He follows part of the law of the by-product in earnestly seeking to do a good job and not seeking for a sign. However, unless he meets the other two laws of spirituality, this alone is not likely to incur a blessing.

His activity might be interpreted as meeting the law of adventure. However, he seems content to settle for things he can plan and organize himself. There does not seem to be a great deal of venturing forth into the unknown beyond his depth.

There cannot be much fruit of the Spirit if there is not much spirit.

b. **Describe how it meets, or fails to meet, the four steps to healthy spirituality in this session.**

Max seems to have lined himself up with God to a limited extent but for reasons we discussed in the law of need, he did not push very far on that. He has done a good job of taking on a responsibility. However, he did not search very far for the eternal dimensions in that responsibility or he would have found a number of other things his members urgently needed to have done for them. However, because of the lack of searching for deeper needs and the lack of adventure, this is more like an efficient business operation than a leap of faith.

c. **Describe what some dangers are if the person continues the present course.**

If Max continues on this course, he probably will have a crackerjack volleyball team. It is not likely the group will have many outstanding growing experiences or a deep and rewarding sense of fellowship.

d. Describe what that person should change to improve the chances of a healthy spirituality.

Max needs to struggle with the eternal dimensions of his job. He needs to be sensitive to the many needs of the members and the opportunities for growth and service. As Max struggles with the problems presented by this expanded sense of mission, he will grow spiritually and as a leader. The singles group will become much more valuable to its members and the church.

Bertha's Story

a. Describe how it meets, or fails to meet, each of the spiritual principles in session 3.

As long as Bèrtha is so confident of her ability to study everything out for herself, she does not meet the principles of need.

She might qualify on the principle of the by-product in pushing herself to study things out and learn the truth without seeking a sign. However, as with Max, this alone does not qualify for a blessing unless she meets the other principles.

She does not seem to qualify for the principle of adventure in the spiritual sense. While she pushes into the unknown, she does it trusting in books and in her own strength as a scholar. There is no leap of faith with reliance in God.

It is unlikely she meets the principle of good fruit.

b. Describe how it meets, or fails to meet, the four steps to a healthy spirituality.

There is no indication that Bertha takes any of the four steps.

c. **Describe what some dangers are if the person continues the present course.**

Bertha should develop a fine mind and this is good. However, this intense focus can rob her of balanced development. There are times when the brightest of people confront problems too big to handle alone. Bertha may need God's help and be unaware it is available. Also, it is easy to get on tangents or small selfish concerns when God's ennobling influence is not cultivated. Bertha may someday wonder where life is headed, and if it is worth it.

d. **Describe what that person should change to improve the chances of a healthy spirituality.**

Bertha needs to practice the admonition to learn "by study and by faith." She must practice the steps to spirituality so her studies can be for a more satisfying purpose. As she studies there will occasionally be added stimulus and insights available to her. Bertha will then have a needed strength to draw on when human wisdom is inadequate.

THINKING THROUGH OUR FAITH

SESSION 7

KEY CONCEPT: Functioning Partnership

KEY STATEMENT: The challenges of life are easier and clearer if we think through our partnership with God.

OBJECTIVES

At the end of the session you should be able to
1. evaluate personal growth in concepts about God during this course;
2. list some God-given gifts which should be cultivated;
3. suggest ways to help people with a variety of faith problems;
4. describe reasons to be flexible in interpreting past revelation;
5. describe the hazard in this flexibility.

EXPERIENCING GOD'S BLESSINGS

Q 1 *Write your views in each box below.*

At the end of session 1 you wrote views on these same subjects. After completing these statements turn back to those written in session 1.

In pairs discuss each other's feelings about any changes from what was written previously. Why did these changes occur? What does this say about your personal openness to new ideas?

---

a. How ready is God to provide blessings?

---

b. In what circumstances does God provide blessings? What insights from session 3 are especially helpful?

---

c. How can we tell if it is really God acting? What insights from session 5 are especially helpful to you?

All of us have gifts. Few of our gifts are as highly developed as they will be if we work at them. Still, all have particular inclinations and abilities. Each of these gifts is a calling to further develop our unique potential in that direction. This makes it important to recognize our gifts so we can develop them.

Q 2 *List five personal gifts you feel God has given you. After completing the list, discuss them with a partner.*

_____

_____

_____

_____

_____

TOWARD SPIRITUAL MATURITY

Homer grew up in the church and had a strong faith in God and the scriptures. The last few years he found some things in scripture he cannot accept. This has shaken his faith in everything associated with religion. Here are some of the things Homer found in the Bible which disturb him:

- The Apostle Paul sanctioned slavery. He told slaves to be obedient to their masters. He told masters to treat their slaves fairly, but did not suggest they free them.
- God ordered extermination of conquered Canaanites. Homer does not think a just and loving God would do this.
- The creation stories seem unrealistic to Homer.

105

• Isaiah promised ancient Israel a glorious return to Jerusalem after the captivity in Babylon. It actually was a difficult ordeal.

Q 3 How can you help Homer keep these problems from undercutting his faith?

Q 4 What can Homer do to develop a sound faith?

Jennifer is a good choir director and she loves it. She organized and conducts the adult choir, a children's choir, a youth chorus, and a double quartet. She has rehearsals four nights a week, plus special performances. She also spends a lot of time selecting music, planning rehearsals, arranging special numbers, and all the other things that go with managing so many groups. The double quartet sang on the radio three times last year. The youth chorus sang before four community groups. Jennifer loves her music work.

There is one problem. Her husband, Mark, isn't sure he has a wife; her children, ages five to eleven, are not sure they have a mother, and the house doesn't look like anyone cares. The past year the children have become openly resentful of Jennifer's preoccupation with her music. Mark and Jennifer had an earnest discussion last week over her responsibilities and priorities. Mark named several qualified people who would take some of the choirs. Jennifer said, "I'm doing the Lord's work with both my music and my family. I'll turn it over to the Lord to decide what I should do." After private prayer, she felt assured that she should continue her strong emphasis on music. She was cross with Mark for having tried to persuade her to give up some of these jobs.

Q 5 What factors indicate whether or not Jennifer had a genuine spiritual experience?

Q 6 What advice can you give Jennifer in regard to her experience?

Dick Jones, our pastor, asked Dave Smith to be young adult leader. Dave has a couple of good reasons to refuse. He has never been a department leader, and his new insurance agency takes a lot of time. Fortunately, Brother Jones has thought this through. He has three even better reasons for Dave to accept. First, Dave provides an excellent role model. He is the kind of successful, Christian person everyone wants as a friend. Second, several participants are experimenting with activities that spell serious trouble. A wholesome church program with effective Christian leadership is their best chance to work on these problems and protect the rich promise of their lives. Third, there are only six people in the congregation that Brother Jones feels are up to the challenge. While he has not asked the other five, he knows they have better reasons to turn the job down than Dave does.

Dave was deeply touched by the challenge, and the tribute to himself. Dave said, "I'll take the job if God wants me to. I'll think about it a couple of days. If God makes it clear that I should accept, I will."

Q 7 How might Brother Jones respond?

As a girl, Floy had a beautiful faith. Older folk always thrilled to her worship contributions; she had such a sweet and trusting ardor for Jesus.

When she was ten, her school raffled off a new bicycle. Floy thought of all the fun she could have riding it; she imagined how envious her friends would be; she pictured how much her parents would appreciate the errands she would run for them. She prayed very hard for that bicycle. She made God an irresistible deal on the good deeds she would do with it. To Floy's surprise, the bicycle was won by a boy who already had a bicycle. He did not need it and did not particularly want it. This did not seem fair of God. Floy was troubled.

In high school, Floy was good at science and she wanted to become a doctor more than anything else in the world. Her heart was set on getting to college, even though her parents could not afford it. It was very important to her and she could do so much good with her medical training that she knew God would find a way. In spite of all her efforts and prayers, God did not find a way. She began to wonder about God.

The television report on the starving millions in Bangladesh aroused strong sympathy in Floy. She asked God why so many innocent people could be allowed to suffer so much. She prayed for God to end the famine. Thousands continued to die each week. Floy could not reconcile this with her girlhood picture of God.

Last year Floy's mother was injured by a drunken driver. She suffered through extensive surgery and life-saving measures. The family maintained a round-the-clock vigil in her room. Dozens of people offered countless prayers for her. After two weeks of suffering, she died. It was so senseless, so unjust, so unloving. Floy asked, "What kind of God is this?" She has not been to church for three months.

Q 8   What is missing from Floy's story which might explain why her faith did not survive these trials?

Q 9   How might Floy be reassured that God is with her?

Q 10   What spiritual rules should she be cautioned to observe?

\#   Caleb is a research biologist. He does not see much room for God in the scheme of things. He sees a fairly orderly world that is understandable without God. His career and his family are pretty well set. He does not feel much need for God.

Q 11   How might you help Caleb develop a faith in God?

Mildred prayed for Zion for many years. She is disappointed in the progress, but she has faith. She says that in God's due time he will send the spiritual endowment. Then, under God's direction, the Saints will build Zion. Until then all we can do is be pure in heart and wait in faith.

Q 12 What are the flaws in this expectation?

Q 13 What should Mildred be doing to answer her own prayer?

In 1954 President Israel Smith brought instruction that self-sustaining elders should be called to be seventies. In years since this has proved very beneficial. Self-sustaining seventies have greatly increased the church's missionary strength. At that time, however, the presidents of seventy opposed the change because it contradicted previous instruction that seventies should travel continually. Most self-sustaining seventies could not travel that much.

Russell Ralston, then a president of seventy, was one of those most deeply disturbed by this new revelation which contradicted his interpretation of the previous revelation. Russell reports:

I struggled for nine years, unwilling to compromise what I believed to be truth and yet torn by what the church had endorsed as revelation. After the Conference of 1958 I was senior president of seventy. The burden became doubly heavy because it was my responsibility to lead the council in the calling of men to the office of seventy. I lived also under the indictment of an inspired message from President W. Wallace Smith to the Melchisedec priesthood in the closing priesthood prayer service of the 1962 Conference. I can never forget the words—"My servants of the Council of Presidents of Seventy have not been willing to implement the instruction I have given earlier and they are impeding the work of the church."

My years of struggle reached the climax as I approached the December 1963 sessions of the council at which time we had to prayerfully consider selecting men to serve as seventy.

One Wednesday night I sat in prayer meeting wrestling with this

Apostle Russell Ralston ordaining priesthood in Haiti

problem and feeling very bleak. In my mind's eye I saw these words emblazoned across the front wall of the church, "The letter of the law killeth, but the spirit of the law giveth life." Then I was asked, "What is the letter of the law concerning the seventy?"

I answered, "The seventies shall travel continually."

Next the Spirit asked, "What is the spirit of the law?"

I answered, "They are called to be special witnesses." The question came back, "What is more important; that the seventy travel continually or that they be special witnesses? Does one have to travel continually to be a special witness?"

The crushing realization came over me that the new revelation would increase the spread of the gospel and advance the spirit of the law. The new revelation "giveth life." My insistence on the letter of the law, without regard to the spirit, was the destructive force.

Today Russell calls this his "Road to Damascus" experience. It was difficult for a confirmed letter-of-the-law person to realize that a dynamic relationship with God sometimes requires abandoning cherished ways in response to deeper truths. This was also necessary growth to prepare Russell for his later call as an apostle. Particularly, this insight was priceless when he provided leadership in interpreting the Restoration for the culture of Haiti.

Q 14 *What tests could have been applied to this revelation of 1954 that might have helped those who were concerned?*

Q 15 *What might be your attitude toward the earlier revelation that seventies were to travel continually?*

Q 16 *The preface listed two purposes for this book.*
- *To help people maintain a dynamic faith in a time of confusion*
- *To encourage people toward mission as God's partners*

Both purposes were to be accomplished by guidance on how to achieve a fruitful partnership with God.

Now that you have finished the book, what ideas have been helpful on these purposes?

If you wanted to accomplish either of these purposes with a friend, what ideas would you use? How would you use them?

NOTE: There is no author's comment on this question. What matters is what you think (and do).

KEY INSIGHTS

Spirituality is an act of partnership. It is never capricious; it occurs only to further the purposes of the partnership between God and us.

The best way to cultivate a spiritual testimony is to enter into partnership with

God. The divine power will then sometimes enhance our powers if
- there is real need,
- it comes as a by-product to serve a Godly purpose,
- we are engaged in a fresh adventure beyond our capabilities.

When God is involved in an experience
- it does not bear bad fruit. Usually we can detect good fruit.
- it does not result from spiritual snares.
- persons involved will probably sense awe, a craving to respond to God, a quickening mentally and emotionally, and a sound message.

There is powerful appeal in trying to cement personal relationships with God by revering old doctrine or trying to recapture past glories. It is so much simpler and more reassuring to go by the book. Often this brings an emotional glow which can be mistaken for spirituality. However, true spirituality is deadened by a comfortable rehash of the familiar.

Past spiritual experiences, especially those canonized in scripture, are a valuable guide. Prophetic people use these experiences as a base to build from, not a prison into which they are locked.

In meeting needs the Spirit usually deals with today's circumstances, and disciples (even prophets) usually interpret from today's perspective. Thus tomorrow will require new experiences and new interpretations. This is why present-day prophecy and an open canon of scripture are so necessary.

True spiritual experience is a dynamic, risking, contemporary adventure with God. We best sense God with us at the growing edge.

DISCUSSION COMMENTS

1. **Write your views in each box below.**
   a. **How ready is God to provide blessings?**
      As was discussed in session 1, God is always available to provide blessings of any needed variety. However, as discussed in session 3, this is guided by principles. These are discussed in more detail in part *b.*
   b. **In what circumstances does God provide blessings?**
      Session 3 listed the principle of need, the principle of the by-product, and the principle of the adventure which indicate when blessings may commonly be expected.
   c. **How can we tell if it is really God acting?**
      Session 5 lists five spiritual snares which could raise a question about whether an experience is genuinely spiritual. Even more to the point, it describes four evidences of true spirituality: we sense awe; we crave to respond to God's call; the total person is quickened; and the message is sound.

2. **List five personal gifts you feel God has given you.**
There is no right answer. The teacher might list a couple, then encourage others to name some they are conscious of in themselves. Suggest possibilities such as a gift for friendship, forgiveness, understanding, hard work, cooperating, wisdom. After the partners have shared, ask them to name gifts seen in the other. Each one may think seriously about other personal gifts which need to be developed. This can be best done when alone later. Suggest treating each of these as a challenge to partnership with God in cultivating that gift.

3. **How can you help Homer keep these problems from undercutting his faith?**
Trying to refute these arguments probably will not be effective, even though you may find a few flaws. What Homer really needs is a faith that is based on experience with God. Share with him testimonies like those in session 1 and a program for action like session 6. When he has experienced God working in his life, he may be able to profit from the Bible stories which make sense to him without being too disturbed by those with which he has difficulty.

4. **What can Homer do to develop a sound faith?**
Session 6 lists four steps: line up my purposes with God; take a responsibility; search for the godly dimension in that responsibility; and make the leap of faith. Other things might be considered like hearing persuasive testimonies. There is no assurance that this or any other system will actually develop a sound faith, but these four steps are the

surest way to develop a sound working relationship with God which can lead to stronger faith-building experiences.

5. What factors indicate whether or not Jennifer had a genuine spiritual experience?

Session 5 offers help on this. There seems to be a real possibility Jennifer may have pushed herself into assuming her arguments for continuing the music were spiritual to justify her desires. This snare does not require any insincerity. Because she so wanted that outcome, she should be cautious in attributing the thoughts to God.

There may be some escapism and desire for recognition in her passion for the musical groups. However, those do not seem to be spiritual snares in her case. She did not use the spiritual experience itself to escape or to gain attention. She merely used it to justify her desires.

When looking at the evidences of true spirituality, it becomes even more evident that Jennifer did not have a spiritual experience. There is no evidence that she sensed awe. She did not crave to respond to God's call. God's love did not trigger her love or expand her wisdom. She was not drawn above her narrow partisan ambitions. On the contrary, she was hostile toward her husband for trying to draw her from her partisan ambitions. Magnanimity and impartial concern for all the values involved in the situation would have been stimulated in a true spiritual encounter. This was missing in Jennifer.

This next point could be debated, but a case could be made that the message was not sound. When Jennifer's heavy involvement was taking such a toll on her family, and there were others who could take over part of the load, the wisdom of her "spiritual" message is questionable.

6. **What advice can you give Jennifer in regard to her experience?**

She could be alerted that whenever an experience confirms what we most want it to say, we need to be especially cautious in assuming God said it. It is very important for her to sensitize herself to the impact on her family, and on other workers who might profit by sharing some responsibility. Then she should pray for the Spirit to quicken her love and wisdom, to lift her above the fray so she can see the issues more clearly. Such a prayer is more effective than merely asking for an answer. She needs to shift from seeking confirmation of a specific idea to seeking the divine perspective.

7. **How might Brother Jones respond?**

He might explain that people who wait to undertake a responsibility until the Lord tells them to do it understand spirituality backwards. Spiritual experience normally is what happens to help us as we are actively engaged in the problems of life or the Lord's work. Our most significant experiences normally come after we have moved out in faith on a worthwhile endeavor. Apply the principle of the by-product from session 3.

8. **What is missing from Floy's story which might explain why her faith did not survive these trials?**

The story does not indicate a working partnership with God. God seems to be the heavenly grandfather she goes to for favors. This does not encourage meaningful experiences or a durable faith.

9. **How might Floy be reassured that God is with her?**

Positive testimony from others may help Floy. It might help even more to point out that she has been too passive in her relationship with God. Commonly the greatest blessings are to magnify the powers of active partners, rather than to give rewards to those who ask.

As with most others, Floy's best reassurance comes if she accepts the challenge to active discipleship.

10. **What spiritual rules should she be cautioned to observe?**

Floy should be challenged to try the four steps to a healthy spirituality in session 6: line up with God; take a responsibility; search for the godly dimension in that responsibility; make the leap of faith. It would also help to inform her on the principles of spirituality in session 3.

11. **How might you help Caleb develop a faith in God?**

All the other people we talked about wanted a faith. The problem was to show them how. Caleb poses a bigger problem: he is not interested. He may be stimulated by the dream of building Zion. He might sense a need for God to stimulate such a wonderful thing. It is probable that scriptural authority and appeals to logic will fail to persuade Caleb of God. Direct testimonies about God by his friends may whet his interest. Direct experience with God is probably needed to convince him. This will take careful and insightful nurture.

It may be impossible to help Caleb develop a faith until problems in life persuade him he needs help.

12. What are the flaws in this expectation?

The spiritual endowment will not come by waiting, even with pure and faithful hearts. Most spiritual blessings will come as the faithful move beyond their depth in serving God.

13. What should Mildred be doing to answer her own prayer?

Get busy. If 10 percent of the members are working effectively for Zion and 90 percent are waiting with Mildred, a 10 percent Zion will result.

Instead of praying for Zion, she should pray for herself and her friends to have the energy, wisdom, and devotion to be Zion-builders. If she acts on that prayer, then her prayer is effectual and some progress may occur.

14. What tests could have been applied to this revelation of 1954 that might have helped those who were concerned?

First, all those who were considering the matter should have been careful of the spiritual snares in their interpretation. In this particular case the most dangerous ones were probably pressure from the congregation (in this case their quorums), and justification of their desires. In such cases they must try to wash their minds of partisan interest before approaching the problem. In fairness we should assume some of the leaders involved did this.

In considering the revelation of 1954, each person

should have sought divine light which exhibited the four evidences of true spirituality listed in session 6. Russell Ralston's "Road to Damascus" experience met all four tests. However, the spirit he felt prior to that was deficient in the second (God's presence did not trigger his love or wisdom or yearning to immerse himself in the spirit he felt) and the fourth (the message was not sound). It would have helped if all had sought spiritual enlightenment which met the tests before taking a position.

15. **What might be your attitude toward the earlier revelation that seventies were to travel continually?**

In considering the prior revelation, the seventies were justified in taking it seriously. It had been carefully considered and was recognized as inspired when adopted. It had served the church well.

However, it is rarely wise to make past instruction into a prison beyond which growth cannot occur. Conditions change and different instructions are required so that the universal principles of the gospel may be effectively served today.

In session 4 the filtering process of the human mind (even the prophetic mind) in fully comprehending the mind of God was discussed. Even the prophetic scriptures are human approximations of what was originally experienced with God. One reason for the church's belief in continued revelation and an open canon of scriptures is this requirement to keep refining and reinterpreting past instructions.

When confronting two conflicting revelations we cannot take the easy way and assume the oldest is correct—therefore the new must be wrong. Our calling is more demanding and more productive. We are called to cultivate the gifts of discernment. We can then evaluate new instruction in the spirit Russell Ralston was able to use after his "Road to Damascus" experience. We will then be freed to progress in a way not possible if we either blindly revere past prophecy or reject it.